At the Foot
OF THE
Father

*60 DAY DEVOTIONAL WALKING
TOWARD A LIFESTYLE*

*MICHAEL & RACHEL
FERGUSON*

Contents

Introduction

I am sure there are some that sit down with the intention of writing a book, but that was not our intention. As we dove deeper into studying God's Word and preparing to receive the truth and insight God would share, what began to happen was a need to capture what we were learning. The next step was to write down what we learned, so that it could be shared with others. We started by creating single page PDF files that we could upload to our website and make available to anyone who wanted a daily devotional. As the number of the devotionals grew it became more appropriate for us to consolidate them into a single location, and here we are.

At the Foot of the Father was written to take you to that place, the foot of the Father. Have you ever sat and listened to someone share their story, their creation, their passion, or their love with you? These and many more are what God is sharing with us in the Bible. Every time we read His Word and prepare our hearts, we sit at the foot of the Father, actively engaged in conversation with Him, listening to the Spirit inspired truth of the one true God. If you are new to the Bible or you are thinking about God as a person you can talk to and with, we want you to know that God desires that kind of relationship with you, and He is waiting for you to take that step.

As you read a devotional, we pray in just those few moments each day, you will begin to feel God's presence, His still small voice. That voice that calls from inside of you, telling you that YOU matter, that YOU are enough, that YOU are wanted, that YOU are loved, that YOU were fearfully and wonderfully made on purpose and for a purpose! You were made to change this world with God leading your path, to shine His light into a dark world. So, close your eyes, imagine a warm arm around your shoulders and see your protector, comforter, savior, counselor, friend . . . Father, sitting with you and getting ready to share His story of which you are an important part. Pray for the Holy Spirit to fill your heart and open you up to hear the Word of God and share what you learn. We are not called to be passive; we are called to be active. Share the Word, share the light of God, and make a daily encounter at
the foot of the Father a lifestyle not just an appointment. God Bless You. Now. Let's talk to the Father!

Trust in God

"Trust in the Lord with all your heart, and do not rely on your
own understanding; in all your ways know Him and
He will make your paths straight."
Proverbs 3:5–6 (CSB)

PRAYER

Heavenly Father, teach me to trust you, and have confidence in your will and the path where you are leading me. Help me, Lord. Help me live a life that brings you glory and demonstrates what trusting in You looks like. Amen

SONG

"Trust in You"
by Lauren Daigle

Finding Peace During Pain, Loss, or Fear

Habakkuk 1-3, Philippians 4:6-7

Philippians 4:6–7 "Don't worry about anything; instead pray about everything. Tell God what you need and thank him for all He has done. Then, you will experience God's peace, which exceeds anything we can understand. His peace will guard your hearts and minds as you live in Christ Jesus."

Whether you were raised in the Church, or you have never been in a church, you have likely heard the phrase, "peace that passes understanding." It comes from these verses. However, if we are unable to understand this type of peace then the question becomes how we get it, especially in times of pain, loss, or fear. Simply being encouraged, "not to worry and to pray about everything" when we are in those moments does not always help. However, you can be assured that it is possible! No matter the situation you are in, God can give you peace.

The prophet Habakkuk gives us an example of how to find peace during pain, loss, and fear in the Old Testament book that bears his name. The society around Habakkuk was increasingly violent, no one followed God and there was no justice. Everywhere he looked, he saw injustice because those in charge were corrupt. There was an economic divide. The rich were getting richer, and the poor were getting poorer. The rich also stole from the poor with no repercussions. On top of all of that they had just been conquered by Egypt, and the Jewish people were now regarded as a lesser class of people. In these circumstances of pain, loss, and fear, Habakkuk prays to God and pleads for Him to deliver His people. God answers Habakkuk's prayer by telling him He (God) has the plan to help Israel. He is going to send the Babylonians to conquer them.

Wait, what? As you can imagine Habakkuk is not pleased with this response, and questions God's very character. How can God send the wicked to destroy them and remain quiet while it happens? God is pure and good, yet He is going to use evil to bring justice? God answers Habakkuk again and explains that the righteous will live by faith in the hope He gives, and even though God may use a corrupt nation for His justice it does not mean he endorses them. They too will fall to His justice.

After God's second response, we see Habakkuk go from anger and fear to a "peace that passes understanding." In Habakkuk 3, we are given a template for praying to God and finding peace in these moments. First, he appeals to God to continue His work and praises God. Then he remembers the awesome power of God and moments where God has delivered them in the past. It is through this praise, and remembering the faithfulness of God, that Habakkuk reaches a point of peace that we see in 3:17–19. Even with the Babylonians still coming to bring God's justice, Habakkuk can sing joyful praise to God because he trusts that God's righteousness will prevail. He will find strength in the promises of God, he will find hope, he will find peace!

So, peace is possible. Habakkuk found it with destruction still on the way. We just need to follow his example to bring it forward to God and trust that God has a plan, and His righteousness and faithfulness will prevail. We can do that because God said the righteous would live by faith in the hope He gives. Whether you are dealing with loss, pain, or fear, turn it over to God, remember what he has done for you, and trust that he has a plan. Peace is available to you during pain, loss, or fear because He is God, He loves you and He has a bigger plan. We need to trust in Him.

A Faith that Changed Everything

2 Kings 5

People will often say that God will use ordinary people to do extraordinary things, which is true. We can see examples in David, the shepherd boy that was not even considered a possibility to be king by his father because he was the youngest and not as strong as the others. God used David, and David became the greatest king in the history of Israel. He also used David, as a boy, instead of the thousands of soldiers available, to defeat Goliath. Another key figure is Mary, a young teenager who was to give birth to Christ. He used Gideon, from the tribe "that was the least of all tribes and of which he was the least," to deliver Israel. From these chosen people, we also see a difference in their faith. Their faith made them available to be used by God from the beginning, David and Mary would both be examples of ones with strong faith. However, Gideon was used after having to be convinced that he was chosen, but then his faith made him available. Another inspiring story of an ordinary person being used by God to do extraordinary things involved a young woman whose faith was stronger than 500 years of Jewish tradition.

This young girl's story begins when she is taken from her home in Israel to Syria to be a slave. She is taken to the home of Naaman, who was the commander of the army of the King of Aram. While Naaman was a brave soldier and in a position of power, he also suffered from leprosy. This was a debilitating disease, and if he could not be cured, then his life, as he knew it, would have to change dramatically.

This young Israel girl, however, knows something that Naaman does not. She knows the ONE true God. She knows that God could heal Naaman, and so she speaks up. "She said to her mistress, 'If only my master would see the prophet who is in Samaria! He would cure him of his leprosy'" (2 Kings 5:3, NIV). She was speaking about the prophet Elisha a man renowned for his connection of prayer with God.

Let's pause here for a second to understand a little more about the character and faith of this young woman. She was taken from her home, taken to a foreign land, turned from a free woman to a slave, and yet she offers a solution to those who captured and ripped her from her home and life. When you live a life of faith and obedience to God, putting all your trust in Him, your faith in God can be seen in how you treat people, even when things appear unpleasant and make no sense.

She believed God could heal Naaman, a non-Jew. This is extraordinary because no Jew had been healed from leprosy since the time of Moses, over 500 years earlier! That was when leprosy happened due to Miriam's sin, and later she was healed. So, this young woman believed God would heal a non-believer, when he had never healed a Jewish person of the disease. She believed it strong enough to stand up and tell her captor, her master, how he could be healed. And Naaman was!

We all have it in us to be used in extraordinary ways by God; we just need to be available, and put our trust in Him. Every day, no matter the circumstance, when we fully put our trust in God, the love for others flows from us. Perhaps God will use you like he did this girl, to demonstrate His power through your faith and do something that had not been done for 500 years and would not be done for 800 more. That time, by Jesus himself.

1 Samuel 17

In the famous Broadway play *Hamilton,* we hear the main character Alexander Hamilton sing a specific phrase repeatedly in a song entitled "My Shot." In the chorus Hamilton exclaims, "And I am not throwin' away my shot, I am not throwin' away my shot, Hey yo, I'm just like my country I'm young, scrappy and hungry and I'm not throwin' away my shot." Hamilton was standing up for what he believed in and was not going to just sit on the sidelines and watch others fight for freedom. He was going to take his shot; he was going to enter the battle.

The first time I heard this song I immediately thought of the story of David and Goliath in 1 Samuel 17. Can you hear David singing this as he walks toward Goliath? I am not giving away my shot! When David arrived at the battlefield, he was shocked to see all the Israelites hiding in their tents. They were all hiding from Goliath, a literal giant. Goliath, the Philistine, was standing between the two sides, the Israelites and Philistines, representing the Philistine army, and daring anyone to come and fight him. He was not just standing; he was trash talking. He was insulting the one true God, and yet the chosen nation of Israel hid in their tents instead of standing up to Goliath. For forty days in a row, Goliath made a stand, and Israel hid. When David arrived at the front and heard Goliath, everything changed.

At the time, David would have been about 15 years old, not old enough to join the army, but old enough to shepherd sheep. In those moments alone amongst the sheep, we learn that David not only fended off many animals but defeated a lion and a bear. He knew how to fight, and he knew where his strength came from. His strength came from the Lord. While the others considered their strength insignificant compared to Goliath's, David knew that God would prevail because God's strength is greater than all others.

I wonder how the other men felt as this 15-year-old boy called them out for their lack of faith. Did they feel relieved that someone would fight Goliath, and that it did not have to be them? Were they still scared? Were they upset with David because he called them out? They hid for forty days, and in the first hour David was there, he prepared to fight in the name of God.

The King offered David his armor, but David did not accept it. He would enter the battle against the armor clad nine-foottall giant with his normal shepherding clothes and a slingshot. He would pick up five smooth stones for the fight. Why five? God did not tell David how many would be required, only that Goliath would be defeated. Also, David would need to be prepared if others came to Goliath's aid. However, we know it took one shot. It took one stone to defeat Goliath. It took one stone, and faith in the power and promises of God! Why did David succeed where others failed? Because his faith was not in himself but in God to win the victory. He brought the ultimate weapon!

What are you facing in your life that scares or intimidates you? What is your Goliath? Have you prayed about it? Are you going to fight? Have you asked God for His strength and deliverance? Are you going to give away your shot? God will always be with you in the fight, when you call on him. Another great line from the song "My Shot" states, "when you are living on your knees, you rise up!" See your Goliath, put your faith in God, go to your knees, pray, and TAKE YOUR SHOT!

I Just Need More Willpower

Romans 7:17-20, 1 Kings 4:29-34, 1 Kings 11:1-8

How many times in our life have we believed, that if we just had enough willpower, we could overcome an addiction or a sin we frequently fall into? Perhaps you have even prayed to God to give you more will power, yet you still fall time and time again. It is frustrating and exhausting to fail repeatedly. Did you know even the biggest heroes of the Bible struggled with this same issue? Take Paul for example. He shares this exact feeling in Romans 7:17–20.

"But I need something more! For if I know the law, but still can't keep it, and if the power of sin within me keeps sabotaging my best intentions, I obviously need help! I realize that I don't have what it takes. **I can will it, but I can't do it**. I decide to do good, but I don't really do it. I decide not to do bad, but then I do it anyway. My decisions, such as they are, don't result in actions. Something has gone wrong deep inside of me and gets the better of me every time. (MSG)"

Paul was not alone in this struggle, but the difference is Paul realized the attack came in the spiritual realm. The enemy was constantly fighting to bring Paul down; when

Paul relied on his own will, he failed. The same happened to another man, the wisest man to ever live, Solomon. Blessed by God with unmatchable wisdom, Solomon still fell to his pride and reliance on himself, rather than the strength of God. 1 Kings 4:29–34 tells us he was the wisest man in the world, and he was famous all across the world for his wisdom. He could speak about plants, animals, birds, reptiles, and fish. He spoke 3000 proverbs and over 1000 songs. From every nation, people came to listen to his wisdom. However, all that knowledge and wisdom would not keep him from failing and turning from God. It wasn't instant; it was over time, a slow fade of temptation and sin that Solomon's will could not overcome. Without God's strength and reliance on God's will, Solomon fell.

1 Kings 11:1–8 shows the work of the enemy defeating the willpower of Solomon. It started with Solomon's lust for women and the enemy used this lust to infiltrate Solomon's home and heart. He was even warned of the impending sin in verse 2. "You must not marry them, because they will turn your hearts to their gods." However, Solomon did not listen and took 700 wives and 300 concubines. Is there any doubt he thought he could handle it?

As he got older his wives "turned his heart to worship other gods instead of being completely faithful to the Lord his God (v. 4). He built altars to other gods, adn worshiped other gods. Solomon "did what was evil in the Lord's sight" (v. 6). Do you see the influence of the enemy? He used Solomon's lust for women to introduce other gods into Solomon's life. He built altars for the gods that these women worshipped, and in the end he started worshiping with them at these altars. The man blessed with the most wisdom in history *'could not will'* himself past the sin of lust, then the sin of idolatry that followed.

The enemy is on the prowl like a lion ready to devour you (1 Peter 5:8). The attack is relentless and in your own will, you will not win. You need to rely on the strength of God to defeat the enemy. Pray without ceasing and put on your spiritual armor, every day. No matter how strong or wise you are, you need God to claim victory. Just like Paul and Solomon, you will fall from time to time, but Jesus will never fail. His victory has already been won! Go to God and let it be His will, not our own in the battle.

Seeing the Victory

Psalm 3, 2 Samuel 15:17-22

There are times in our lives when we feel like everything is against us. We feel like there is no way out of the situation that we are in, and there is no chance that it is going to get any better. The Bible is full of men and women experiencing these same feelings, so what can we learn from one of their examples? Let us look at King David as he put this struggle to verse in Psalm 3.

Understanding the backstory of this Psalm is important to help us better comprehend David's struggles and his perception that everything is going against him. David is on the run, at this time, on the run from the army of his son Absalom, who is trying to kill him and take over the throne. Absalom had killed his brother Amnon, who had raped their sister Tamar. After having Amnon killed, Absalom fled and was away for two years. During this time Absalom grew bitter and began wanting the throne for himself, and upon his return he began usurping the throne.

He used his influence as the king's son to get the people on his side. He did this by taking their side without investigation as they waited in to talk to David about their concerns (2 Sam. 15:3–6). He then spread lies throughout the twelve tribes that he was the king of Hebron. He also convinced David's strongest counselor to leave the king and become his advisor. At this point, Absalom's power and influence were so great that David fled for his life, fearing that an attack could fall on Jerusalem if he remained. (15:14)

It is here, while he is fleeing, that the Psalm begins. "O Lord, I have so many enemies; so many are against me. So many are saying, 'God will never rescue him!'" (Psalm 3:1–2). It was a tough time for David, his own son wanted him dead, but David knew that he was not alone, he knew God was with him. "But you, O Lord, are a shield around me; you are my glory, the one who holds my head high. I cried out to the Lord, and he answered me from his holy mountain." (3:3–4)

David starts this prayer with praise to God. God is his protector, even while being chased by the enemy. All that David has is due to God, it is his because of God that David has accomplished what he has, and it is God who holds him up during times of struggle. It is God that will give him rest and peace to be able to press forward. "I lay down and slept, yet I woke up in safety, for the Lord was watching over me. I am not afraid of ten thousand enemies who surround me on every side." (3:5–6).

David put his faith in God, and even when all seemed lost, he prayed to the only one who could get him through, God! Did you notice the difference after God gave him rest, and after he poured out his heart of faith to God? David awoke with confidence in what the Lord was going to do. No longer was David in fear. God had conquered his fear. David knew he could put his full trust in God to defeat the enemy. He relied on God, not himself, which gave him strength and courage.

"Arise, O Lord! Rescue me, my God! Slap all my enemies in the face! Shatter the teeth of the wicked! Victory comes from you, O Lord. May you bless your people." (3:7–8). David was ALL IN! He stood strong in the strength of the Lord! And, when we put our full trust in God, and give over to Him all that surrounds us, then we too can know victory when all seems lost. It is time to go ALL IN!

When You Cannot See Purpose Through the Pain

Exodus 1:15-2:10, Lamentations 3:19-26

We have all been through times in our lives that are painful, sometimes physically and sometimes emotionally. During those moments we know that we must pray and lean on the strength of God to get through, to persevere. Often, we will have friends send us a prayer or a verse to help lift our spirits. Perhaps Romans 8:28 (NIV), "And we know that in all things God works for the good of those who love Him, who have been called according to his purpose." But what are we to do when the pain is so overwhelming we cannot see the purpose?

She was a young mom when the new law went into effect. She had a beautiful young daughter and a son, plus she was about to give birth to a second son. Then a command to kill the infant if it was a boy was given to the midwives who were assisting in the delivery of all the births. Being God-fearing women, the midwives did not listen to this command, so the command was issued again. Only this time the command was given to everyone to throw any newborn son into the river to drown. When her son was born, she disobeyed. She would not throw him in the river, but she would have to find a way to hide him from everyone. Anyone that knew of his birth could turn her in and the baby would be taken and killed.

Can you imagine the fear this young mother was living with every day? It was known she was pregnant, and then one day, she was no longer pregnant. There was no baby girl; thus, the child must have died at childbirth or had been a boy who was dumped in the river all these would have been what everyone thought. She would have to find ways to stifle the baby's cries so they would not be heard or discovered. She would do this for three months; however, a choice had to be made as she could not hide this child forever. She had to make the most painful decision a mother would ever have to make. She had to take a chance that the very family that put the law in place, would be the ones to save her son.

So, she waited until the moment when the daughter of the ruler who enacted the law was bathing in the river; she put her three-month-old son in a basket and floated him to her. The pain of loss must have been tremendous, as would have been the fear of knowing if it would even work. Even as the child floated down the river death was not an unexpected outcome. While the child was saved, he would now be raised without her. She likely could not see God's purpose in this situation through her pain.

By now, you may realize this is the story of Moses. We have the benefit of knowing the whole story and knowing that not only would God save Moses from death, but He was going to use Moses to free all of Israel from Pharaoh. There was a purpose to all this pain, Moses, a Hebrew child raised in Pharaoh's home, would have access to Pharaoh as no one else could, to be God's voice.

When you are unable to see the purpose through the pain, that is when you need to trust the most. Remember what it says in Lamentations 3:22–26, "The faithful love of the Lord never ends! His mercies never cease. Great is his faithfulness; his mercies begin afresh each morning. I say to myself, 'The Lord is my inheritance; therefore, I will hope in him!' The Lord is good to those who depend on him, to those who search for him. So it is good to wait quietly for salvation from the Lord." Looking back, we can see God work to comfort Moses' mom, while working towards his purpose, even if she could not see it at the time through the pain. God was there. He is always there. Trust in His mercies every morning and in His promises even when they cannot be seen through the pain.

Overcoming Adversity

"Here is what I am commanding you to do. Be strong and brave.
Do not be afraid. Do not lose hope. I am the Lord your God.
I will be with you everywhere you go."
Joshua 1:9 (NIrV)

PRAYER

Dear Jesus, I need you. I feel overwhelmed, and burdened with the obstacles in my life, and I am exhausted by the constant daily struggle. I don't know how to turn the chaos over to you, please show me how. Take it from me Lord. Let me wake up refreshed and renewed by your strength. Amen

SONG

"Praise You in This Storm"
by Casting Crowns

Where Is God When I Am in the Storm?

Have you ever had moments of chaos in your life? Moments when it feels like everything that could go wrong not only will, but will to an extreme level? When life's storm becomes overwhelming, relentless, and unbearable. You begin to wonder if you will ever find your way out. God feels absent, nonexistent, like He does not notice or care about the storm in your life! However, nothing could be further from the truth. God not only cares about you, but He also loves you! You are not alone. We often wonder why bad things happen to good people, or to us as Christians once we have asked Jesus into our lives. Shouldn't this be the point where God intervenes to end the chaos, and calm the storm? Where is He? Isn't He supposed to protect and prosper us as believers, yet here we are, struggling through this raging storm in our life?

There are many stories in the Bible of believers suffering in both the Old and New Testaments. Paul speaks of the suffering he endured as a believer in Christ, and there are references of him being beaten nearly to death, being imprisoned, and dealing with a constant "thorn" in his flesh (2 Cor. 12:6–7). Yet,

Paul speaks of this through the lens of JOY. Peter also speaks of suffering in 1 Peter 4:16 (HCSB), "But if anyone suffers as a Christian, he should not be ashamed but should glorify God in having that name." So, suffering will happen, and storms will occur, but that still does not answer the question of where Jesus is during the storm.

To answer this, we turn to one of the most famous stories in the Bible. The story of Christ walking on water. In Matthew 14:25–32, the disciples are on the Sea of Galilee when a major storm hits. They are in trouble, and Jesus is not with them. In the middle of the night, in the darkness, during the raging storm they see Jesus walking towards them on the water. They are scared and not sure if it is Jesus or a ghost. Peter speaks up in verse 28. "Lord if it's really you, tell me to come to you, walking on the water." So, Jesus calls Peter out of the boat during the storm, but as Peter takes his eyes off Jesus and focuses on the storm he begins to sink. He calls out for Jesus to save him, and Jesus immediately reaches out and saves him.

We should never miss this point: Jesus is there reaching out to save us when we call out His name. Often, we do not realize Jesus is all we need until we are at that moment when Jesus is all we have, as Peter experienced. However, it is not just what Jesus did at that moment, but it is what He did not do that answers our question. He did not calm the storm! Yes, He saved Peter, but we see what happens next in verse 33. "When they climbed back in the boat, the wind stopped." Jesus waited until He and Peter walked back to the boat, climbed in the boat, and then the storm stopped. Even though Peter was saved out on the water, the storm still raged, but Jesus walked with him back to the boat, and then He calmed the storm in Peter's life.

We were never promised that the storms of life would end once we believed or if we were a "good" person. We are promised that Christ will save us when we call out to Him in faith. We are promised that while He may not end the storm, He will walk us through it! We simply need to call out to our Savior, and reach out to Him. He will save you, and walk with you through the storm. And, did you notice, the storm was no longer the story once Peter held on to Christ?

You Are Not Alone in the Fire

Daniel 3

While there are many great stories in the Bible that demonstrate the power of faith and the awesomeness of God, perhaps one of the best is the story of Shadrach, Meshach, and Abednego. These three young men took a stand against a king, and the result of that stand would have them cast into a fiery furnace. Death was not only guaranteed, but it would be torturous. So, where was God during all of this?

The story began in Judah, when the Babylonians laid siege to the city, took captive the best young men from Judah and brought them back to Babylon to serve in the king's court. Among these captives were Shadrach, Meshach, and Abednego (Dan. 1:6–7).

Once they were in the court, King Nebuchadnezzar had a massive gold statue made of himself, and set it up in a place where all could see it every day. And how could they not see it? It was 90 feet tall and 9 feet wide, made of shimmering gold (Dan. 3:1)! The advisors to the king decided that during the dedication ceremony for the statue they would announce that every time music was heard that every person would be required to fall in worship to the king. If they did not do this, then they would be thrown into a fiery furnace and die (Dan. 3:4–6).

Our three heroes in this story were Jewish, and even though they served in the court of King Nebuchadnezzar, they only served the one true God and would worship no one or nothing else. As a result, when the music began, they did not bow, which drew the attention of the king. So, Shadrach, Meshach, and Abednego would have to answer to the king for not bowing to his golden image in worship.

One of my favorite verses from this passage is their response to the king, when they are told if they do not worship the idol, they will be thrown into the furnace. "If we are thrown into the blazing furnace, the God we serve is able to deliver us from it, and he will deliver us from Your Majesty's hand. But even if he does not, we want you to know, Your Majesty, that we will not serve your gods or worship the image of gold you have set up" (Dan. 3:17–18, NIV).

The king was so angry he ordered the furnace to be made seven times hotter than normal. It was so hot that even the soldiers that threw our heroes into the fire were consumed by it. However, when the king looked into the furnace, he saw four men in there not three. The king realized that the fourth in the fire was sent to rescue Shadrach, Meshach, and Abednego. They were walking around in the furnace unbound and unharmed, and when they came out their clothes had not burned, and they did not even smell of fire. So, the king praised the one true God for saving the lives of these three men (Dan. 3:19–28).

Their faith had saved them, and it changed the world, but even if God had not intervened, they still would have refused to worship a false god. It is not that they wanted to die and be thrown in the furnace; it was that they trusted God. They trusted that whatever the outcome, God would be with them. And He WAS!! So, whatever the fire is in your life right now, there is one thing that is certain. If you put your trust and faith in Jesus, then He will be with you in the fire. You are not alone! That is the promise we have from God, and this is one of many examples that prove it! Trust in Him, He will not fail you! Live in your faith and watch God change not only your circumstance, but also the world!

Can You Carry More with a Full Hand?

Are you ever overwhelmed by your to-do list for the day? Do you notice it often falls into four categories: House, Family, Job, and Extra? Those can be broken down into more detail; however, look at the overriding themes of your list. Do you find yourself struggling to balance how these four areas must be completed in a day? What happens if more are added? What happens when you need to help someone else? Do you catch yourself reaching your tipping point?

So, imagine you have four themes of tasks on your to-do list for the day. How do you balance each of those if you need to accomplish 100%? Let's balance at 25% and look at them as 4 fingers of a hand. If you used 4 fingers of your hand to "hold on" to your day, how long could you hold on? Can you hold on to anything if you don't have your thumb? You can, but not well. What if you consider YOURSELF as the thumb and put YOURSELF on your daily task list? Consider these your primary 5 tasks in a day. You need your thumb to hold everything together. Without time to fill your Spirit in a day, you will drop things, too. Fill yourself with the Spirit to find peace.

Solomon states in Ecclesiastes 4:6 (NIV),

"Better one handful with tranquility than two handfuls
with toil and chasing after the wind."

Isn't that how we all feel? If we cannot take care of ourselves and the life around us: our own self, family, house, job, and tasks at home, how can we begin to take on more? Doesn't it become a juggling act? Don't we get to the point of burnout? What if we never keep the task list within the primary five?

So how do you look at YOUR 5? Where are YOU on that list of care? If we are called to follow Jesus and go and make disciples in the Great Commission of Matthew 28:16–20, when are we able to help others if we are tipping over with our primary 5? Step 1: We must define where we put Ourselves and get our mind, body and spirit filled. How long has it been since you prayed, listened to music or took time to walk/sit in a quiet place and just listen to God?

2. Define how much you should give the other primary 4? Is it the majority of your time? Would you say the scale is balanced?

3. How much do you reach out to help others? Galatians 6:2 (BSB) says, "Carry one another's burdens and in this way you will fulfill the law of Christ." We all know that if we focus on something other than what we cannot get completed, then we forget about our worries, and that small change can free us to help someone else through their own. It feels good. Did your mom ever tell you that when that math problem is hard . . . just walk away and return to it? It makes your head clearer. You see the solution, or at the very least receive calm from the strain.

So again, I ask, how can you carry with four fingers? If you have two full hands, how can you find peace? As God tells us, "My yolk is easy and my burden light," Matthew 11:28–30.

Where are you making your burden heavy? Where have you taken too many tasks into your hands? Where have you forgotten to take care of your "thumb"? Prioritize the time to be filled up by God. Look at your primary 5. Rebalance your list. Put yourself and your time with God at the top of your list. Then look to unload and live with one hand open to help those around you.

Where is God When I Am Scared?

. . . .

1 Kings 19:11-13

There are times in our lives when fear grips us, and even getting out of bed or taking that next step seems impossible. During these times, you have probably asked yourself: Where is God when I am drowning in my fear? Is God gone? Why can't I hear Him? Does He even care?

First, let me assure you that God not only cares about you but also loves you. However, the enemy will use fear to separate you from God. To make you desire to be isolated, to pull back from friends, family, and faith. You find yourself retreating into your own cave of darkness, and the fear seems stronger and inescapable. The more the enemy makes you feel alone, the stronger the sense of fear grows, the more silent it seems the voice of God becomes, and the more we continue to isolate ourselves. So, how do we battle fear? How do we listen for God?

Psalm 46:10 (NIV) "Be still and know that I am God . . ." A verse we hear from our Christian friends and even see on shirts, signs, and pictures. Well, if you are like most of us, you may be thinking, "Great, but what does that mean and how do I do that?" The great news is that God provided us with an example of a person living through tremendous fear, and how that person finally heard the voice of God. That person is the prophet, Elijah.

Elijah had just witnessed God defeating the false prophets of a false god in an amazing display of His power. Yet Elijah was suddenly filled with fear for his own life despite the utter defeat of the enemy, so he ran! The story begins in 1 Kings 19, where Elijah is running in fear for his life. Elijah had just called on the name of the Lord to deliver fire from heaven and fear now causes him to run instead of calling on God for help. After many days of running, he ends up alone in a dark cave in a mountain. He is alone, fear is winning, he cannot hear God,

and he retreats deeper and deeper into his cave, isolating himself more and more. Then something happens; as Elijah moves away from his fear and listens, God speaks! But not in the way you may expect.

"The Lord said, "Go out and stand on the mountain in the presence of the Lord, for the Lord is about to pass by." Then a great and powerful wind tore the mountains apart and shattered the rocks before the Lord, but the Lord was not in the wind. After the wind there was an earthquake, but the Lord was not in the earthquake. After the earthquake came a fire, but the Lord was not in the fire. And after the fire came a gentle whisper. When Elijah heard it, he pulled his cloak over his face and went out and stood at the mouth of the cave. Then a voice said to him, "What are you doing here Elijah?"

—1 Kings 19:11–13 (NIV).

God did not shout or yell, He spoke in a whisper. It required Elijah to come to the mouth of the cave, quiet his soul and listen for the whisper. God had not abandoned Elijah in his fear, but the enemy had made him feel that way. Just as the enemy is making you feel that way. Quiet your heart, quiet your mind, pray and listen. God wants to speak to you in your heart, comfort you and help you through the fear, but we must meet God at the mouth of our caves to hear him over the chaos of fear. You cannot do it alone; you need God to defeat fear. He is passing by your cave, are you ready to trust, to be still, and to know He is God?

Soaring on the Strength of God

Isaiah 40:28-31, 2 Cor 12:9-10

An often-quoted passage in the Bible comes from Isaiah 40:28–31. "Have you never heard? Have you never understood? The Lord is the everlasting God, the Creator of all the Earth. He never grows weak or weary. No one can measure the depths of his understanding. He gives power to the weak and powerless. Even youths will become weak and tired, and young men will fall exhausted. But those who trust in the LORD will find new strength. They will soar high on wings like eagles. They will run and not grow weary. They will walk and not faint."

When we study chapter 40 of Isaiah, what we find is the reminder that God is the creator of the world. The king of the world and His power, authority, and wisdom are without limit. This was important for the nation of Israel because they were currently in exile. Many probably felt abandoned by God, or at the very least; they were discouraged about their future. This was made clear in verse 27, "O Jacob, how can you say that the Lord does not see your troubles? O Israel, how can you say God ignores your rights?" They were complaining about the difficulty of their circumstance. They were questioning where God was and why He was not delivering them.

Have you ever felt like the Israelites? Have you been so overwhelmed by the difficulty or adversity you were facing that you complained to anyone and everyone? Have you felt that God does not care about your pain or what you are going through? If you have, then welcome to the club. We have all had these moments, which is why this passage is so important. It really can be your life verse reminding us that God is above all things in power and authority, and that he has also granted His supernatural power to those who believe! How does he do this? He does this through his strength flowing in and through us.

Consider the eagle in this verse. When an eagle takes off for flight it flaps its wings powerfully to take off and then rises in the air. However, this is not the image we are being given in this passage. Isaiah tells us that those who trust in the LORD will SOAR on wings like eagles. When an eagle is soaring, there is no flapping of their wings. Their wings are outstretched as far as they can reach and then what happens next is truly a beautiful comparison of what we can do when we face adversity. The eagle uses the wind that is blowing against it, rising up against it and uses it to lift itself HIGHER!

Do you see it? The eagle uses the adversity blowing directly into its face, trying to take it down and turns it into the very things that causes it to SOAR! This is what Isaiah is saying to the Israelites in chapter 40 and to us today. Even in those moments when we become weak and tired in the battle, when the stress and adversity seem too much to handle, when we are exhausted to the point that we cannot go on, God's supernatural strength enables those who believe, who TRUST to overcome the hardship. Not just overcome, but to rise and soar on wings like eagles!

The same promises that were made to Israel thousands of years ago are still true for you today. God is with you and His strength will raise you up. "Each time he said, 'My grace is all you need. My power works best in weakness.' So now I am glad to boast about my weaknesses, so that the power of Christ can work through me.   For when I am weak, then I am strong" (2 Cor. 12:9–10).

Spiritual Warfare

"A final word: Be strong in the Lord and in his mighty power. Put on all of God's armor so that you will be able to stand firm against all strategies of the devil. For we are not fighting against flesh-and-blood enemies, but against evil rulers and authorities of the unseen world, against the mighty powers in this dark world, and against evil spirits in the heavenly places."

Ephesians 6:10–12 (NLT)

PRAYER

Dear Lord, today I claim victory over the enemy by putting on the full armor of God. I put on the belt of truth that I may stand firm in the truth of your Word. I put on the breastplate of righteousness that it may guard my heart against evil and keep me protected under the blood of Jesus Christ. I put on the shoes of peace that I may stand firm in the Good News of the Gospel so your peace will shine through me. I take up the shield of faith to protect me from Satan's fiery arrows of doubt, denial, and deceit. I put on the helmet of salvation that I may keep my mind clearly focused on You, Christ, confidence in my salvation, and not the lies of this fallen world. I take up the sword of the Spirit that may it be strong in my hand that I may expose the lies of the enemy. And I pray without ceasing that by faith, I, your warrior, will live this day in spiritual victory! Amen.

SONG

"Surrounded (Fight My Battles)"
by Michael W. Smith

The Demon of Lack and Limitation

Exodus 4:10, Judges 6:15, Matthew 9:20-22

Spiritual warfare is real and is constant. We are protected by the armor of God (Eph. 6:10–18), but even so we are reminded to be alert to the schemes of the enemy as he is constantly on the prowl waiting to destroy us (1 Peter 5:8). One of the demons the enemy uses frequently and effectively is the demon of lack and limitation! We need to be alert to its presence.

What is this demon? This is the demon that whispers to you to convince you that you are not good enough to be saved by Christ. That you do not have the faith or the ability to live a life pleasing to God, or that you are not talented enough to be used by God or to serve Him. Do you see the enemy's scheme? The enemy is trying to take you out of service to God and out of relationship with God; his goal is to separate you by whispering lies into your insecurities. You are not alone; this happened to some of the greatest heroes of the Bible.

Exodus 4:10 tells us that after God spoke to Moses from a burning bush, and said to him that he would speak for God; however, Moses still believed he was not the right candidate because his speech was limited (many believe Moses had a stutter). Moses was being chosen by God, and God was telling him he was enough, yet the spirit of limitation caused Moses to pause.

In Judges 6:15 (NIV), we find Gideon hiding in the bottom of a wine press threshing wheat when an angel appears and tells Gideon that God is going to use him to lead Israel over the Midianites. Lack and limitation are all over Gideon's response, "how can I save Israel? My clan is the weakest in Manasseh, and I am the least in my family." Do you see it? Sound familiar? Abraham thinks he is too old. The prophet Jeremiah believes he is too young, as does Timothy in the New Testament. Lack and limitation are everywhere today and, in the Bible, even when God speaks directly to us with a calling.

However, when we rely on the strength of God, the power of His Word, and hold onto our faith, we will prevail. Isaiah 54:17 tells us that no weapon formed against us will prosper, so the enemy will not win unless we allow it. We are victorious! One unnamed hero of the Bible demonstrates the power of Christ over lack and limitation. Her story is found in Matthew 9:20–22. Three verses that show overwhelming victory over lack and limitation.

This woman is suffering from a bleeding disease but has faith that Christ can heal here. However, she also is being whispered to by lack and limitation that she is not worthy enough to ask Jesus directly, maybe even that she does not deserve healing. However, her faith is so strong that she knows if she just touches the robe of Jesus, she will be healed, and that is exactly what she does. And that is exactly what happens!

Lack and limitation could have kept her away, after all that is the goal, to keep us from Christ. Her faith brought her to Christ, and through the strength of Christ the enemy was defeated, and she was healed. You have this same opportunity.

Do not let the whispers of the enemy lead you to believe you lack or are limited in any way. Cast it off and know that "I can do all things through Christ who strengthens me" (Phil. 4:13, NKJV). Christ has already won the battle. We need to trust, pray, and enter the battle with the strength of Christ. Remember, "Greater is He who is in you than he who is in the world" (1 John 4:4, BSB).

As a Believer, are there Ghosts?

Ephesians 6:10-12

The TRUTH is "we are not fighting against flesh-and-blood enemies, but against evil rulers and authorities of the unseen world, against mighty powers in this dark world, and against evil spirits in the heavenly places" (Ephesians 6:12).

So spiritual warfare is at hand. Before you begin to break down whether there are ghosts or spirits in this world, you must have a basis for understanding the battleground: Light vs. Dark. We must define Light and Dark. We have to parallel Light with Good and Dark with Evil. It is biblically written that acts of the flesh (worldly darkness) are sexual immorality, impurity, debauchery, idolatry and witchcraft, hatred, discord, jealousy, fits of rage (anger), selfish ambition, dissensions, factions, envy, drunkenness, orgies, and the like. But the fruit of the Spirit is love, joy, peace, forbearance, kindness, goodness, faithfulness, gentleness, and self-control. (Galatians 5:19–23). Paul goes on to note that those who believe in Jesus Christ (Believers) have crucified the flesh (desires of darkness) and life in the Spirit by staying in step with the Spirit (v. 25). Without a reference point of good/Light, then there is no barometer for defining evil/Dark.

The Bible states, Evil was cast out of Heaven to rule of this Earth. Revelation 12:7–12. That still does not answer the question, are there spirits in this world?

We can learn the answer from Jesus, He cast out demons (spirits) on many occasions, even moving them from people into pigs in Matthew 8:28–34. So, there are spirits, but do spirits only interact with Jesus? No. The disciples also cast out spirits. In Luke 9, Jesus gave them the power and authority to cast out all demons and to heal all diseases in His name. Jesus himself tells us of this power in John 14:12 (NIV), through the connection with the Spirit, "I tell you that whoever believes in me will do the works I have been doing, and they will do even greater things than these, because I am going to the Father."

Being one in the Spirit is said by Paul to include the spiritual gifts listed in Romans 12 and 1 Corinthians 12, which include teaching, prophecy, laying of hands, speaking in tongues, and discernment. Even the prophet Joel is referenced in Acts 2 that the Spirit will be poured out on all people causing daughters to prophesy, young men to see visions and old men to dream dreams.

God has advised us to Stand Firm in our faith, and walk by faith, not by sight. Yet, the enemy must flee in the name of Jesus. Whether you believe this spiritual authority and gifts only occurred during Jesus's time, or you experience dreams that become a reality, or have seen the touch/hug of a friend remove sadness, or pain, or provide complete healing. I can state through my own experience, beyond a shadow of doubt, that the gifts of the Spirit are at hand and working in the world today. If we believe there is Heaven, we must believe that there is Hell; therefore, we must educate ourselves to walk within the spiritual battle of this world.

The spiritual world IS present. However, do not take my word for it, but Ask Jesus to answer your question! Jesus tells us, Ask, and it will be given to you: Seek, and you will find. Matthew 7:7.

NEVER FORGET, the enemy must flee, in the name of Jesus: James 4:7. We must walk with Him and use Him to fight the battles in front of us. It is through His authority not our own that we battle in the spiritual.

Are You Prey?
or Will You Pray?

1 Peter 5:8, Ephesians 6:10-18, Isaiah 54:17

Could you imagine living under the constant risk of being devoured by a lion? Wondering if around every corner the lion was waiting, or if every sound you heard was the lion approaching. You realize you are not safe during the day or at night; even being in a group offers no guarantee. This was the life for the men that built the Kenya-Uganda railway in the Tsavo region between March and December 1898.

During those nine months two man-eating lions hunted and attacked the men building the railroad, killing as many as 135 men according to some reports. These lions came to be known as the Tsavo Man-Eaters. During those nine months the attacks became more and more brazen. It could happen during the day or at night. Even being inside your tent did not protect you from attack. Could you imagine the strain and stress on these men? Always on the alert, wondering if they were next to be devoured. The one advantage they had was the danger was visible; they could see it coming. As Christians we are in a similar situation, only that our danger is not visible, our danger is in the spiritual realm, but it is still a lion!

"Stay alert! Watch out for your great enemy, the devil. He prowls around like a roaring lion, looking for someone to devour." 1 Peter 5:8

The greatest trick the enemy ever pulled was convincing the world that he does not exist. The reality is, however, the enemy *DOES* exist and is looking to devour you like a lion, to destroy you! Maybe it is through temptation that slowly builds to a sin that separates you from God, isolates you from loved ones, and leads you to lose everything you care about. Maybe it's a quick, bad decision that has consequences that destroy earthly relationships, or even steal your freedom, and separate you from God.

So, what can we do? How can we fight the lion? Without God, we cannot! We need to believe in Jesus Christ as our Savior and accept Him into our hearts. Once we genuinely believe in Jesus Christ, we are given protection against the enemy from our Lord and Savior. We can be strong in the Lord, in His power. Eph. 6:11 (NIV) tells us, "Put on the full armor of God, so that you can take your STAND against the devil's schemes." We fight in a battle that is not flesh and blood, it is a battle against the *"powers of this dark world* and against the spiritual forces of evil in the heavenly realms" (Eph. 6:12, NIV). So, we need to armor up! We take our stand against the enemy!

We take this stand by putting on the belt of truth, the breastplate of righteousness, and the boots of peace. We take up the shield of faith, put on the helmet of salvation, and take up the sword of the Spirit, which is the Word of God (Eph. 6:13–17). And we PRAY! On all occasions PRAY, be alert and always keep on praying (Eph. 6:18)!

With Christ you have access to the armor of God. So, be confident that when you believe, you can STAND, because you

STAND in the strength of God! The enemy may be PREYING to devour you like the lions of Tsavo, but we can stand against those schemes by being alert (1 Peter 5:8), and prepared (Eph. 6:10–18). Do not believe the lie; the enemy does exist, he is waiting to devour you. However also know that no weapon formed against you will prosper (Isa. 54:17). It may be formed against you, but when you trust and rely on Christ, it will not prosper. Christ will be victorious, and the battle will be won, but until that day, stay alert, take a stand, and do not be *PREY*, but instead **PRAY** on all occasions in your battle!

Oppressed or Possessed?

John 16:33

How do you define being oppressed or possessed? As a believer in Jesus Christ, do you even speak of these words? Does the thought of possession enlist fear or concern? Have you ever considered the difference between the two, and what it means for a believer in Jesus? Let us start first with a clear understanding of both. Webster's Dictionary defines possession as the condition of having or owning, or controlling something. Oppression is defined as the state of being subject to unjust treatment or control. While there are examples of possession by demons in the Bible and it does still occur, we more often see oppression by the enemy compared to full possession.

Do believers experience either? Let us go all the way back. As believers in Jesus Christ, we live in a broken world and are guaranteed we will have trouble. (John 16:33). We have knowledge of good and evil by Eve and Adam's partaking of the apple in Genesis 3. From that sin and exercise of free will, the toiling of life began.

The first step in this battle is a choice. You must choose.

Do you want to believe in Jesus Christ? Do you believe He is the way, the truth, and the life (John 14:6)? Second, do you believe He came to rescue you from sin? As a believer, you must come to acknowledge that evil exists (Gen. 3) and that anything evil does not dwell within God (Psalm 5:4). Satan, however, is out to kill, steal, and destroy (John 10:10). He prowls around like a roaring lion looking for someone to devour (1 Peter 5:8).

As believers, we must fight to free ourselves from satan's oppression, which limits our ability to live and serve Christ. As followers of Christ, we have the Holy Spirit dwelling in us (Rom. 8:11). We must recognize the actions that do not align with the fruits of the Spirit; love, joy, peace, patience, kindness, goodness, faithfulness, gentleness, and self-control, (Gal. 5:22–23), is of the devil working to OPPRESS you. The Holy Spirit, however, does not oppress you. The Holy Spirit comes and fills you, dwells within you when you surrender your life to Jesus and follow Him, and out of the Spirit flow the gifts of the Spirit. (John 16:7, 1 Cor. 3:16)

If you do not believe in Jesus Christ, what you connect to will determine how you live. You can be POSSESSED with any spirit or idol by which you believe, thus succumbing to that spirit's control and losing your own control. However, you have the freedom of choice to decide which higher power you believe in. The choice is yours alone.

If an eternity in Heaven is your goal, then there is simply one way to get there. You must choose Jesus. Christ is the only way to Heaven (John 14:6). Accept Jesus into your life and become filled by the Holy Spirit. Come to live and learn to remove the oppression Satan tries to lay on you to limit you from your full potential in Jesus Christ (Eph. 6:11–12).

No longer do you have to live in fear or belief that it is not possible to achieve relief. It may not be easy to overcome oppression; on your own, you cannot, but Christ can overcome all oppression! The enemy has no choice but to surrender to Jesus Christ. "Therefore, God exalted him to the highest place and gave him the name that is above every name, that at the name of Jesus every knee should bow, in heaven and on earth and under the earth, and every tongue acknowledge that Christ is Lord" (Phil. 2:9–10, NIV). You can choose what fills, oppresses, or possesses your spirit. You can seek to understand the truth of what oppresses you if that is where you are suffering. But remember, Jesus has already won the victory and the enemy must flee in the name of Jesus (James 4:7). Take a stand in the name of Jesus and Fight!

Living in the Fruit of the Spirit

"But the fruit the Holy Spirit produces is love, joy, and peace. It is being patient kind and good. It is being faithful and gentle and having control of oneself. There is no law against things of that kind. Those who belong to Christ Jesus have nailed their sinful desires to his cross. They don't want these things anymore. Since we live by the Spirit, let us keep in step with the Spirit. Let us not become proud. Let us not make each other angry. Let us not want what belongs to others."

Galatians 5:22–26 (NIrV)

PRAYER

Heavenly Father, everything I have been given comes from you. You are my source of all things good. I come to you today asking for a supernatural touch to help me live a life filled with the fruits of the Spirit. Help me to love, to be full of joy, peace, and patience. When I am with others help me to be kind, gentle, good, and faithful. And help me live a life of self-control that I may bear fruit that others see, and that when they see it, they see You. Amen.

SONG

"Holy Spirit Come"
by Patrick Mayberry

Living in Purpose

1 Corinthians 12:8-11

You have a purpose and a destiny that only you can fill.

Psalm 139:2–3 (NIV)—You know when I sit and when I rise. You perceive my thoughts from afar. You discern my going out, you Lord, know it completely.

"For I know the plans I have for you," declares the Lord, "plans to prosper you and not to harm you, plans to give you a hope and a future." Jeremiah 29:11 (NIV)

Whether you are Gideon and need to really be convinced God is asking you to do something: Judges 6, or you are Paul and you will give everything, even your life, to share the gospel: Acts 20:22–24.

God calls everyone that believes in Him to help others and share the Good news.

Feed the hungry and help those in trouble. Then your light will shine out from the darkness, and the darkness

around you will be as bright as noon. Isaiah 58:10
He has placed inside of you gifts.

To one there is given through the Spirit a message of wisdom, to another a message of knowledge by means of the same Spirit, to another faith by the same Spirit, to another gifts of healing by that one Spirit, to another miraculous powers, to another prophecy, to another distinguishing between spirits, to another speaking in different kinds of tongues, and to still another the interpretation of tongues. 1 Corinthians 12:8–10 (NIV).

Those gifts can be served on Sunday, but they are ideally fulfilled EVERYDAY. Every day, you have someone around you less fortunate than you. Someone who looks up to you. Someone that is being guided by you. Have you ever looked at that? Even Jesus spoke of the parable of being a shepherd that left the 99 to find the one. Matthew 18:12

God has called each of us to share the gifts he has placed inside us.

So, what do you do really well? What comes "naturally" to you? What is a skill you have that you can share with someone? Is it cooking a meal for someone? Is it writing a card or making a call to someone? Is it volunteering at a local food pantry?

1 Peter 4:10 tells us that within each one of us we have a God given gift that is meant to be used to bless others.

Each day we are on this Earth, we know we are one step closer to going home to be with Jesus. If it's not today, then how have you used today to the best of GOD'S ability within you? Remember that Holy Spirit's resurrection power that He has given you? Bring yourself, or someone near you, one step closer to finding the joy in the life they have been given.

Not sure where you are gifted? Find out.

1. Take personality questionnaire: Enneagram, MyersBrigg, CVI, DISC, Spiritual Gifts test
2. Sit down and list what is EASY for you to do, and brings you enjoyment, when you do it.
3. Find someone in your life to sit down with you and talk through questions 1 and 2.

As followers of Jesus, He asks: Matthew 28:16–20:

- You ACCEPT Him as part of your life

- You MAKE DISCIPLES, which means bringing others to know and learn about Jesus

- You TEACH them to obey all he has commanded, which means sharing the good news.

We all can do it. Just take the step to live in your natural gifts. Be that for someone.

See your purpose, LIVE on purpose, and GIVE on purpose, TODAY!

Not So Spooky Spiritual Gifts

John 14:6, 12, 1 Cor. 12:8-10, 2 Tim. 3:16, Matt. 25:31-46,
Luke 10:18, Gen. 3, Rom. 8:11, Eph. 6:10-18,
James 4:7, Prov. 13:20

Are you the one who always hears a "bump in the night!"? Do you catch yourself feeling temperature changes in the room around you? Do you feel like you see things that no one else seems to see? Did you know that you *can be* a BELIEVER in Jesus Christ and have these experiences?

The Bible tells us that Spiritual gifts: increased faith, gifts of healing, the gift of miracles, prophecy, the discernment of spirits, speaking in tongues, and interpretation of tongues performed in the Bible can and still do happen today. In fact, Jesus spoke about this very thing!

"Very truly I tell you, whoever believes in me will do the works I have been doing, and they will do even greater things than these, because I am going to the Father" (John 14:12, NIV). Jesus not only healed the sick, performed miracles, and raised the dead, but also cast out demons. The apostle Paul also speaks to these gifts. "To one there is given through the Spirit a message of wisdom, to another a message of knowledge by means of the same Spirit, to another faith by the same Spirit, to another gifts of healing by that one Spirit, to another miraculous powers, to another prophecy, to another distinguishing between spirits, to another speaking in different kinds of tongues, and to still another the interpretation of tongues" (1 Cor. 12:8–10, NIV).

Before we begin to understand our gifts, we must agree on some key foundational truths. First, Jesus is "the Way, the Truth and the Life. No one comes to the Father, except through me (Jesus)" (John 14:6, NIV). Second, the Bible is the God breathed Word of God given to man (2 Tim. 3:16). Third, there is a Heaven and Hell as mentioned in many passages, including Matthew 25:31–46 and Luke 10:18. "And they will go away into eternal punishment, but the righteous into eternal life" (Matt. 25:46, BSB). "I saw Satan fall like lightning from Heaven" (Luke 10:18, NIV). Another foundational truth is the acknowledgement of Adam and Eve having eaten from the Tree of the "Knowledge of Good and Evil" (Gen. 3). As a result, the acknowledgment of angels and the performance of miracles must also lead to an understanding of what is opposite to goodness, evil.

So, as we agree on these truths, we can then know that the power of the Spirit is available to us today, and lives inside us just as it did in Jesus. Biblically, we are advised by Paul that the same resurrection power that raised Jesus from the dead is living within you (Rom. 8:11). You have gifts of the Spirit provided with a connection to the Holy Spirit.

So, our Spiritual gifts may still seem spooky, but you can know with peace, that even when we encounter spirits of evil, God provides protection: A suit of armor and awareness to the battles in front of us each day (Eph. 6:10–18). You have been given authority over the spirits. You have the power to get the enemy to flee in the name of Jesus (James 4:7).

So, how do you learn to connect to your spiritual gifts?

1. Connect to your source, your Heavenly Father
2. Pray to God, and begin to read the Bible
3. Connect with someone who believes in Jesus Christ and teaches the Word in alignment with biblical truth. Through prayer and sometimes fasting, which Jesus also did, you will get answers. Who you surround yourself with defines where you grow (Prov. 13:20).

As a believer, you are on the winning team. You will make mistakes, but you have the capabilities to walk and perform skills just like the apostles. You must grow in your skills, your connection with God and your faith to believe it is possible. The world needs you to walk in your God–given gifts and use them to share the Good News! Do not fear the bumps in the night, instead, step into your gifts and the power and strength of the Holy Spirit!

You are Saved, but Have You Changed?

If you are saved, are you changed? That question is one we must all answer at some point. We spend much of our time working on salvation, and we should. We pray for our friends and family to be saved and to get to know Jesus. We have outreach events to reach others for Christ. This is all important because without salvation, there is no relationship with Jesus. There is no connection to God, and no hope or rest on the horizon.

However, we often fail to realize that salvation is not the end of the journey, but the beginning. Once we have been reconciled to Christ and are saved through his redeeming sacrifice, the journey and the real work begin. This is when we delve deeper into our relationship with Jesus and grow to know him better. This is where the fruits of the spirit (love, joy, peace, patience, kindness, goodness, faithfulness, gentleness, and self-control—Gal. 5:22–23) flow from the work we are putting into our walk and the Holy Spirit living in us. So, the question we must ask ourselves is, "I am saved, but have I changed?"

One of the characters we meet in the New Testament is essentially asked this question about a situation he is about to encounter. In the book of Philemon, we get to see this all play out. While it is only one chapter in length, it is rich in lessons for all of us.

Philemon was a wealthy man and a new believer and follower of Christ. It is to him that the Apostle Paul is writing this letter. One of Philemon's slaves, Onesimus, had stolen from Philemon and had run away. Onesimus ran all the way to Rome to avoid being found, but because of that choice he met Paul. Paul led Onesimus to Christ, and now Onesimus has a tough decision to make, and Philemon would have to respond.

Onesimus had stolen from his former master and deserted him, so as a follower of Christ, he must return to Philemon and ask for forgiveness and return what he stole. However, this is not an easy choice because Philemon would be legally well within his rights to beat Onesimus and potentially even kill him. But if Onesimus indeed is saved, then he must allow the Spirit to work in him and flow through him, so he must go back.

Philemon is in an interesting position, so Paul is writing to him. Philemon was saved during one of Paul's missionary journeys around Ephesus. So, Paul knows he believes in Christ and that the Fruits of the Spirit should be working in him. So, he is asking Philemon to forgive Onesimus, not just forgive but welcome him back as an equal, not a slave. Paul is counting on Philemon to not only be saved, but also to be changed. The fact that this book is in the Bible suggests that Philemon did just as Paul asked and forgave and welcomed Onesimus back. Could you have done that? Could you not only forgive someone that stole from you but welcome them back as an equal? If you were Onesimus, would you trust God enough to protect you when you knew that being beaten would be an expected and legal response?

What we learn through this letter is forgiveness, kindness, gentleness, peace, patience, and self-control. If we are saved, then the Spirit can change us, and we can not only forgive those that wronged us but welcome them back fully like the brother or sister in Christ that they are.

69

Growing in Our Walk

"In view of all this, make every effort to respond to God's promises. Supplement your faith with a generous provision of moral excellence, and moral excellence with knowledge, and knowledge with self-control, and self-control with patient endurance, and patient endurance with godliness, and godliness with brotherly affection, and brotherly affection with love for everyone. The more you grow like this, the more productive and useful you will be in your knowledge of our Lord Jesus Christ."

2 Peter 1:5–8 (NLT)

PRAYER

Lord, you have called us to grow in our faith, to increase our understanding of our Savior Jesus Christ and to develop a closer relationship with You. This is the desire of my heart, and I pray I come to know You more every day. Thank you for your Word. Thank you for the indwelling of the Holy Spirit. Your Word helps me understand the truth and the Holy Spirit guides me on the path where I should go. I pray that I will learn to walk in the spirit and truth so that I may grow in my faith as I study the Bible and learn to live a life in Christ Jesus. Amen.

SONG

"Nobody"
by Casting Crowns

The Growth of Faith

Salvation is the beginning of our journey with Christ. It is the step where we surrender our lives to Him as our Lord and Savior. It is an exciting, joyful, exhilarating, life-changing event but what comes next? After we give our lives to Jesus, and then display this commitment through water baptism, how do we grow in our faith and relationship with Jesus Christ? We know that the Bible is to be our instruction manual for living a life of faith, but it is large, and at times, overwhelming. So, in this devotional we look at a small Bible passage that demonstrates how we can grow in faith.

2 Peter 1:3–11 begins as if someone has just asked Peter the very question, "How do we live a godly life?" "By his divine power, God has given us everything we need for living a godly life. We have received all of this by coming to know him, the one who called us to himself by means of his marvelous glory and excellence" (2 Peter 1:3). In our surrender to Jesus as our Lord we are given all we need because the Holy Spirit is now with us. The Spirit will work on us by prompting us, with a feeling, when we should change what we are doing because it

would not be pleasing to God. We have also been given God's Word to go with the Holy Spirit.

"And because of his glory and excellence, he has given us great and precious promises. These are the promises that enable you to share his divine nature and escape the world's corruption caused by human desires" (1:4). We find these promises in the Bible. However, as we read the promises of God and what he wants for our lives it is important that we respond to those promises, and in the next few verses of this passage Peter gives us seven ways we can do this.

"In view of all of this, make every effort to respond to God's promises. Supplement your faith with a generous provision of moral excellence, and moral excellence with knowledge, and knowledge with self-control, and self-control with patient endurance, and patient endurance with godliness, and godliness with brotherly affection, and brotherly affection with love for everyone" (1:5–7).

Peter is telling us that we grow our faith by responding to the promises of God with moral excellence. We are to live a life of noble character. We are to seek knowledge; specifically, knowledge focused on Jesus Christ and has a practical purpose of us becoming more like Christ. We are to live a life of self-control or self-restraint over our lusts and passions in life. We should demonstrate patient endurance which simply means we should trust in God in all situations. So, our endurance is united to and flowing from our trust in God. We pursue godliness, to be more like Jesus and we do this not alone but through kindness, generosity, and care for everyone, or with brotherly affection and we demonstrate love for all.

"The more you grow like this, the more productive and useful you will be in your knowledge of our Lord Jesus Christ . . . So . . ., work hard to prove that you really are among those

God has called and chosen. Do these things and you will never fall away" (1:8–10). Peter is telling us we have a responsibility to live our life for Jesus. Jesus chose to save us, but we are responsible to act on his gift of grace by living a life of moral excellence and love as we walk towards the final goal of eternity with Jesus! When we work every day to know Jesus more and be more like Jesus, we GROW in our Faith, which is what living a godly life after salvation means, GROWTH!

Prioritizing Our Time

Psalm 90:12, Proverbs 2:6

If you have grown up around the church, then you would have heard about tithing. It is a Biblical principle about giving God your first ten percent. This is typically discussed around giving God ten percent of what you earn. In the Bible, this could mean the first ten percent of your crops or the best ten percent of your flock. It was important to give God the first fruits of their labor. However, have you ever considered that tithing should include more than simply your finances?

On one of the early dates for Rachel and me, she posed a question to me that I had never considered. "Do you tithe your time?" I had to be honest and quickly admitted that I did not. I thought that was where the questions would stop, but the next question hit harder. "Will you tithe your time?" I instantly became defensive. How could God expect that? Where can I find two hours of my day to give to God? What would that even look like? Am I supposed to spend two hours praying and reading the Bible? I already tithe my income isn't that enough?

Clearly not one of my proudest moments; fortunately, God had seen fit to bring someone into my life that would not just challenge me but had the grace to accept my brokenness. Over the next few days, I began to work on tithing my time, and while the Bible does not specifically have a verse for tithing our time, there are many that indicate the importance of spending time with God. For me, one jumped to the front of the line for the importance of tithing my time for God. "Teach us to number our days carefully so that we may develop wisdom in our hearts." (Psalm 90:12, CSB)

Our time on this earth is just a blip on the timeline of eternity. So, as the Psalmist was pointing out, it is important that we learn to "number our days" to make the most of the time we have been given each and every day in order to gain "wisdom" in our hearts. Where we gain that wisdom is in our relationship with God. "For the Lord grants wisdom! From his mouth come knowledge and understanding." (Prov. 2:6)

My problem wasn't just not understanding I could tithe my time, my problem was I thought of my time as my own. Did you see that in my response? "Where can I find two hours of my day to spend with God?" I was thinking about my work responsibilities, my kids, and the things I enjoy doing each day. Something would have to be given up, but I wasn't sure what I would be willing to part with. That was an eye-opening moment for me. If I truly wanted to live a life for Christ and gain wisdom into how I should live my life for Him, shouldn't my time be something I willingly give? What I had to learn was my time belongs to God. It is a gift He has given me to steward well for Him. It was a hard lesson, that I still miss from time to time.

As you read this, I hope you'll start thinking about how you spend your time. Are you willing to give up more for Jesus? If the answer is no, then you need to ask yourself why? If the answer is yes, then here are a couple of things you can try.

Play worship music or sermons during your time in the car, while in the shower, or when you get ready for work. Pray as you walk from place to place. And always set aside some time to read the Bible, whether in a devotional or directly from the Bible. Our time is His, and we are just giving back ten percent of what he has given to us to steward and belongs to Him. Trust me. He is worthy of our time!

Running The Race

1 Corinthians 9:24-27, 2 Timothy 4:7,
Philippians 3:12-15

Sporting events have long been entertainment for all cultures. It is common to find people watching or attending football, baseball, basketball, or other types of games. Every four years the world tunes in to watch their nation compete against other nations in the Olympics. These athletes have been training their entire lives for this one moment, this one chance to win the race. The apostle Paul helps us see that the life of a Christian and the life of faith is a race to the finish line. So, what can we learn from this comparison?

"Do you know that in a race all the runners run, but only one gets the prize. Everyone who competes in the games goes into strict training. They do it to get a crown that will not last, but we live life to get a crown that will last forever. Therefore, I do not run like someone running aimlessly; I do not fight like a boxer beating the air. No, I strike a blow to my body and make it my slave so that after I have preached to others, I myself will not be disqualified for the prize. Run in such a way as to get the prize." (1 Cor. 9:24–27, NIV)

This passage is focused on self-discipline. For the believer in Jesus, it is focused on our self-discipline in our walk of Faith and following God. There is strict training that the athletes go through to prepare for a race, and the same should be said of us in our desire to *become more like Jesus*, and to *live a life that is pleasing to Him* and brings Him glory. There should be a purpose to how we live our life of faith, just like a boxer preparing for a fight or a runner preparing for a race has a purpose in their training.

We should be spending time daily in the Bible, learning about Jesus and how we should live a faith-filled life. We should be looking for daily opportunities to share what Jesus has done for us in our lives and share his love with others who come across our paths. We should pray and pray continuously, as Paul says, to strengthen our relationship with God, Jesus, and the Holy Spirit. All these will allow us to run the race to our crown that will last forever. That crown is an eternity spent with Jesus Christ in Heaven.

As you think about the need for self-discipline in preparation for running and winning the race, I also want you to picture the end of the race. What does it look like when a runner gets to the end? Do they simply run to the finish line and stop? Or do they run through it? Do they strain and strive for every bit of energy and effort to finish strong? Is this not what we see in an Olympic race? As they approach the finish line, the runners are leaning, straining to cross first, and they run well past the line to ensure they gave it everything they had.

The runners that look behind, before crossing the finish line, to see their competitors are usually overtaken. However, those who strive to the end and only look up after they have crossed the finish line, truly have given their all. "But one thing I do: Forgetting what is behind and straining toward what is ahead, I press on toward the goal to win the prize for which God has called me heavenward in Christ Jesus." (Phil. 3:12–15, NIV) If we run the race with self-discipline, striving to know Jesus more each day, and we run through the end, leaning towards the finish line then we can say, "I have fought the good fight, I have finished the race, and I have remained faithful" (2 Tim. 4:7). And then perhaps we will hear Christ say, "Well done, my good and faithful servant."

We Need Each Other

....

Hebrews 10:19-25

It is becoming clear that society is not only growing further apart, but more isolated. Division is on the rise; unity seems a distant memory and many interact only through technology. Isolation is on the rise! As Christians how are we supposed to live in this world of isolation? Do we need to gather with believers? Is it NOT enough that we have our personal relationship with God? Certainly, we do not need a group of people with whom to worship.

Do you know what makes the lies of the enemy the most effective? It is when he sprinkles in a little truth. Truth: God is enough. Lie: We do not need to worship and live life amongst a body of believers. As we live through the COVID pandemic, this topic is incredibly relevant and will be in the future when isolation again becomes the norm. Hebrews 10:19–25 gives us an understanding of what we should do as individuals and as a body of believers. And it is just as relevant today as it was 2000 years ago.

In this passage believers in Christ are told to take three specific actions. First, draw near to God with a sincere heart

(v. 22). Second, hold tightly to the hope we profess without wavering (v. 23). Third, spur one another on toward love and good deeds (v. 24). The first two of these are individually focused. We are to draw near to God and hold tightly to the hope we have in Him, and do not waver! It is the third action that the church (ekklesia—gathering), the body of believers, is given an action. We are to spur each other on toward love and good deeds. So, how do we spur each other on?

We spur each other on first by "not giving up meeting together" (v. 25, NIV). This was the issue the author of Hebrews was addressing. The church was isolating themselves due to persecution for being Christian. Today, isolation is an issue because some churches have closed, small groups are no longer meeting, and it has become too easy to connect virtually. However, the ability to meet safely has not gone away, and the importance of meeting together definitely has not. We need to be together! We also spur each other on by "encouraging one another" (v. 25). We build each other up, encourage each other to continue to grow, and support each other through difficult times. We stand firm together as a body of believers united under the love and sacrifice of Jesus Christ.

There is joy in giving love, even more than receiving it most times. So, let us be encouragers. Let us dig into the promise, the hope, the love, and the saving grace of Jesus Christ. Let us not give up meeting together. Do not let yourself be alone. Do not isolate. It is too easy to give up, and it is times like these that we need each other even more. Our spiritual growth is not just an individual effort, but a group project. Fear cannot win when we fight together under the name of Jesus Christ.

In Hebrews we are being shown that to grow in righteousness we need each other. So, to all of you I say, you got this!

Fight isolation, and spur on a time of growth: individual growth and growth within your body of believers. If we fight isolation, draw near to God, hold tightly to hope, and spur one another on then we will come out stronger and God will be glorified! Fear is a liar, and we are already victorious. So, stand firm in your armor of God (Eph. 6:10–20).

The Parable of the Good Samaritan

Luke 10:25-37

The parable of the Good Samaritan is one of the most famous of Jesus's parables. There are many lessons that can be learned from this parable. One is clearly that we are to love everyone, regardless of their nationality, ethnicity, etc. That is not a surprise as this is one of the main teachings Jesus always spoke on, loving one another. However, as you read the passage and this devotional, I would like you to focus on, which of these main characters you would be.

Before we get to the three men that passed by the beaten traveler, let us take some time to understand him better. First, we need to understand that Jesus was speaking to a predominantly Jewish audience, while the traveler is not mentioned as Jewish, it would have been understood that he indeed was. This is an important point to note because after he was beaten and stripped, he would have been unidentifiable as Jewish. It was often by how they dressed or how they spoke that the different ethnic groups were recognized. In this case, he was naked and unconscious, so there were no identifiable traits. This is important to the parable.

As Jesus begins his story the audience will immediately realize that danger is a part of the story. The road the traveler was taking was about seventeen miles in length and was well known for being a dangerous road. It would never have been wise to travel alone or even in small groups, as thieves and bandits ruled the road, and robbery was not only common, it was almost expected.

The first person to pass the beaten man is a priest. Clearly, this is a man who should be expected to know God. A priest is someone you would expect to be filled with love and compassion. He was most likely riding on a donkey, as priests were often wealthy, and remember this is a Jewish audience, so this would have been considered a Jewish priest not some false religion. Not only did he pass by without helping a fellow Jewish man, but he steered his donkey to the other side of the road to avoid him!

The next passerby was a Levite. They were like priests because they were professional men supported by their fulltime religious work. It may not have surprised the audience that the priest and Levite passed by the man. They were often viewed as snobbish, and they performed ceremonial works at the temple. If they came in contact with blood, they would be unclean and unable to perform their responsibilities. Although this point could also be argued because the priest was going "down" the road suggesting he was going away from Jerusalem and the temple, not on his way to fulfill his professional role. So these two were unsurprising, but the third passerby would have rocked their worldview!

The Samaritan was the despised enemy of the Jewish people. They were even barred from entering the temple because some Samaritans had polluted the Holy Place. Surely this is not the type of person that would help a beaten stranger. Yet he did. He generously gave time and aid to the beaten Jewish man, his enemy. So, who would you be in this story? Would you need to determine first if the victim is worthy of your care? Would your schedule be more important? Or would you pour out love and kindness regardless of their ethnicity, beliefs, or religion? That is what the parable is calling for us to answer. We are called to love everyone. If any part of your heart holds back love from a group of people, bring it to God and have Him open your heart. Then watch the change and love He can bring to your life, and those around you.

God Desires Men to Lead Their Families

Exodus 4:24-26, Genesis 17:9-14

There are so many interesting stories in the Old Testament of the Bible. Amazing stories of heroes of the faith and God doing extraordinary things through them. One of the most well-known was Moses. In four of the first five books of the Old Testament we learn the story of Moses. We learn how God saved him from death as an infant. We learn how God placed him in the home of Pharaoh to grow up. We learn how God called him to lead the nation of Israel out of slavery. We see Moses acting as the mouthpiece of God, performing miracles and calling on plagues against Egypt in the name of God. We see God give the Ten Commandments to Moses. We see God give the law to Moses to establish righteous living among the Israelites, and we see Moses lead them to the promised land. However, did you know that even with all of those amazing accomplishments, there was a time when God wanted to kill Moses?

In Exodus 4:24 we read that God sought to kill Moses. Some translations read that God attempted to kill Moses; however the original Hebrew word is better defined as desired, wanted, or sought instead of attempted. This desire also came when God sent Moses on his way to be His voice to Pharaoh and free the nation of Israel. At the moment he entered his calling, God wanted him dead! So naturally, two questions come to mind. Why did God want to kill Moses? And what kept God from killing Moses? The beginning of our answers is found in verses 25–26.

We find in these verses that Moses's wife, Zipporah circumcises their son, which keeps God from attempting to and ultimately killing Moses. So why was that so important? What is so significant about circumcising a son that it would keep God from killing Moses? Well for that answer we have to go back to the book of Genesis.

Gen.17:10–14 covers the covenant God made with Abraham and all of the people of Israel. "This is the covenant that you and your descendants must keep: Each male among you must be circumcised. You must cut off the flesh of your foreskin as a sign of the covenant between me and you. From generation to generation, every male child must be circumcised on the eighth day after his birth. This applies not only to members of your family but also to the servants born in your household and the foreign-born servants whom you have purchased. All must be circumcised. Your bodies will bear the mark of my everlasting covenant. Any male who fails to be circumcised will be cut off from the covenant family for breaking the covenant."

God had called Moses to lead God's chosen people out of slavery, yet he had not upheld the covenant with God within his own family. How could he lead Israel for God if he had neglected to lead his own family? Fortunately for Moses he had a wife whose intuition knew what God was requiring and intervened to save Moses. With the covenant fulfilled, Moses became the voice of God for his people, and God used him to accomplish many things for the people of Israel.

For every man who reads this devotional it is time to understand that God has called us to be the spiritual leaders of our family. We cannot effectively lead others until we lead our families in their own spiritual walk. And we must never take for granted the intuition of a woman of God that is by our side.

Power in Purpose

"The Lord will fulfill his purpose for me. Lord, your faithful love endures forever; do not abandon the work of your hands."

Psalm 138:8 (CSB)

PRAYER

Lord, help me to believe your truth that I am fearfully and wonderfully made for a purpose that you had in mind for me even before I was born. I ask you to reveal to me the passions and dreams you have placed in my heart. Reveal to me how these passions and dreams can grow into the expression of the purpose You have for me to make a difference in the world. Direct my path and guide me in using the gifts you have equipped me with to serve others and bring You glory. Fill me with confidence based on who You are and help me trust You so I can have the courage to step into the calling and purpose for which you have created me. Amen.

SONG

"Confidence"
by Sanctus Real

Power in Purpose

There is a powerful impact on your life when you realize you were created on purpose for a purpose. God did not just decide to create you for no other reason than just to live life. You have a purpose! Living in that purpose can change how the world is impacted and how the world impacts you. When we live life without purpose, our circumstances can impact our days, attitude, and direction. When we live life for the purpose that God has given us, we can live a life where our circumstances do not impact us because our purpose is not decided by our circumstances.

For this devotional we will briefly look at two heroes of the Bible who approached life very differently, Gideon from the book of judges and the Apostle Paul from the New Testament. In these two men, you can see the difference when you know your purpose and are living out your purpose as opposed to when your circumstances dictate your days.

Gideon was hiding when an angel appeared to him to tell him of his divine purpose of leading Israel to victory over their enemies. Gideon was unaware of his purpose of leading

Israel, so he hid. He let his circumstances of fear affect how he lived. Even when the angel gave Gideon direction in Judges 6:26 to cut down a pole to a false God, Gideon chose to do this at night for fear of being in danger from those who would be angry. Gideon had not yet accepted his purpose. Even though the angel had shown he was from God and had given him an assignment from God, Gideon still did not buy into his purpose or calling to deliver Israel. He even asked the angel to prove it to him two more times! Judges 6:36–40 outlines Gideon's request for God to prove it, before he would buy it. Once Gideon believed in his purpose and put his life towards that purpose, God showed his power in a mighty way through the leadership of Gideon. Check out Judges 7 to see God defeat the enemy and how he used Gideon. He found power in his purpose!

On the other hand, Paul clearly understood his purpose in life, which was to share Jesus Christ in all he did, daily. Philippians 1 is written while Paul is in jail, but in this chapter, we see the very essence of living out your purpose and the power of that purpose. Paul speaks of his thankfulness first (Phil. 1:7–8) and his hope that the church of Phillipi will continue to grow in their relationship with God (1:9–10). Even though Paul is in chains he considers himself blessed! How can that be?

He is blessed because his purpose is sharing Christ, and that is where he finds his joy, not in his circumstance. The fact that he is in prison is advancing Christ, advancing the purpose Paul was created for and thus he rejoices (1:12–26).

There is power in your purpose! To find your purpose get to know your Father. Spend time in His Word. Ask God to show you your purpose. Then find an accountability partner that will help you live in that purpose. Finally, find ways to share

Jesus every day through your purpose. It may be in the way you live in your corporate job, your family life, it may be in teaching, preaching, or evangelizing. Whatever it is, you can be sure of one thing. God will be in it, He will be a part of that purpose, and He created you specifically to carry it out. You want true joy? Live in the power of your purpose and you will know joy!

There is Purpose in Each Step

....

Acts 9:1-20

There are times in our lives we are confronted with major life events or obstacles that we cannot overcome on our own. Fortunately, for those that believe, we have the love and strength of Jesus Christ to help us get through these times. "I can do all things through Christ who strengthens me." (Phil. 4:13, NKJV). After you come out on the other side of the obstacle, crisis, or event, have you ever looked at all the steps that had to happen for you to make it through? The purpose, complexities and intentionality of God's plan for you at the time, can be found in those steps. For many, these moments are subtle, for some they are hard, but for the apostle Paul, he had to be knocked down.

If you have grown up in the church or spent time reading the Bible, then you would have heard of Paul. He was one of the early leaders in the 1st century church and wrote most of the books in the New Testament. However, did you know that Paul was originally named Saul? Did you know that he hated Christians so much he asked if he could be given the charge to pursue them, arrest them, and even sometimes have them killed? Talk about a change from adversary to an apostle. What major life event could have led to that big of a change? The answer is Jesus.

While on his way to Damascus to arrest Christians, Saul was surrounded by light and fell to the ground. It was here that Jesus spoke to him, "Saul! Saul! Why are you persecuting me?" (Acts 9:3–4). When asked who is speaking Jesus reveals who He is to Saul and tells him to get up and go into the city and he will be told what to do (9:5–6). The problem is that the light had blinded Saul, so those traveling with him had to lead him by hand to Damascus, and he would remain blind for three days (9:7–9).

Now in Damascus, there was a Christian named Ananias. The Lord spoke to Ananias and told him to lay hands on Saul to heal him. This was crazy to Ananias because Saul had been harshly persecuting Christians and arresting them. Surely, it would not be wise to heal Saul. But the Lord told Ananias that Saul had been chosen to be used by God for His purpose. So, he laid hands on him, and he was healed (9:10–19).

As we pay attention to this life-changing moment, we can see God's plan had many steps, and all had a purpose that would be important for Saul to become Paul and be the leader of the church that God created him to be. First, Saul was extreme, therefore, the extreme was required to capture his attention. So, he was knocked down and blinded by the light of Jesus. He needed to be humbled and give up pride and control, so he had to be led around by others. He was helpless to find his own way. Finally, the Christians needed to trust Saul, so God used a Christian to heal him so that it would be clear it was God's plan.

Each step had a purpose. A purpose for Paul, a purpose for those that followed Jesus Christ, and a purpose for us today. All of those can be seen in this life-changing event for Paul, which is not a Paul only occurrence. Looking back at what God has brought us through, we can see purpose in each step. Why is that important? Because you need to always remember that God is there and he loves you so much that "A man's heart plans his way, but the Lord directs his steps." (Prov. 16:9, NKJV). And with each step God has a plan and a purpose. If you make yourself available to Jesus through Him you can accomplish great things in His name, for His kingdom. Are you ready?

The Path Leads Forward

....

Genesis 19:1-26

There are times in our lives when we feel stuck in sin. We feel incapable of finding a way to overcome the same temptations that we fall into on a regular basis. When we hit our low point, it is often then that we reach out to Jesus to save us. That is what Peter did when he was walking on water and started to sink. It was only then that he reached out for Jesus (Matt. 14:30). We know that Jesus can save us, but even when we have that knowledge, it can still be hard to start moving forward. Is it because we feel we have something to prove? Is it because we think we are not important enough for God to save us from our sin? OR maybe it's that sometimes the temptation is so pervasive that we desire to look back on it, even when it has been overcome.

A story in the Bible demonstrates this exact situation for a family struggling to leave behind a place of great sin. It is the story of a man named Lot and his family and their escape from the city of Sodom. The outcry to God against the cities of Sodom and Gomorrah had become so great that God had decided to destroy them both (Gen. 19:13). God sent angels to warn Lot to flee the city and told him to let all his relatives in the city know about the coming destruction.

Lot had a wife and two daughters; these two daughters were to be married, so he quickly ran to their fiancés and told them to escape with them. However, the young men did not take him seriously, so they decided to stay. When the angels were ready to leave at dawn, only Lot, his wife, and his daughters were there. The destruction of the city was about to begin, so naturally you would expect that all four of them would run as fast as they could to escape. Except that is not what happened. Instead, they hesitated. "When Lot still hesitated, the angels seized his hand and the hands of his wife and two daughters and rushed them to safety outside the city, for the Lord was merciful" (Gen. 19:16)

As the angels led the family out of the city, they instructed the family to leave, not to look back, to run for their lives. When sin is involved, when desire is involved, when temptation is involved that command is never easy. This family had hesitated to leave the city they knew would be destroyed. So much so that they had to be dragged out by the angels. Now, they are finally being set free. Set free from a life of sin. Surely, the path forward is the only place they will look, why look behind when freedom was ahead?

Unfortunately, for some, the urge to look back into our sin is too much of a temptation to resist, and so was the case for Lot's wife. "But Lot's wife looked back as she was following behind him, and she turned into a pillar of salt" (Gen. 19:26). Did she really want to be freed from that which bound her to her sin? God wants us to look forward to our freedom in Him not back into the sins that separated us from him and bound us to a life of misery.

Only God can save us. Jesus died to save us from our

sins. Jesus died to save YOU. Just like He saved Peter when he sank in the water, or like God saved Lot from destruction, He can save us if we accept His gift of grace and mercy. The key then becomes moving forward on the path to freedom in Christ and not looking back to the sin that can pull us in. Both Peter and Lot's wife had the same issue, they took their eyes off the Lord and focused on the sin and storms around them, and then they sank. The path leads forward. All eyes on Christ! Trust in Him and be saved!

True Freedom is Found Only in Jesus Christ

Galatians 5

July 4th is Independence Day in America. The day we celebrate our freedom every year. It is a day to remember the sacrifices made, so that we can indeed be a free country. That freedom came at a price, and the freedom we have through Jesus Christ also came at a price. Jesus sacrificing himself for our sins has given us **true freedom** and a purpose in our freedom. "It is for freedom that Christ has set us free. Stand firm, then, and do not let yourselves be burdened again by a yoke of slavery" (Gal. 5:1, NIV).

When Paul is writing this letter to the church in Galatia there is a concern for the new believers that they are not finding freedom in Christ. They are being told that to be saved they must follow the 613 laws of the Jewish people. Remember, at this point Christians are part of the Jewish faith. They have not been separated yet. In this letter, Paul is letting the church know that Christ died to free them from the law and not to make them subject to it.

The law has no place in securing your salvation. It does not matter how good a life you lead; your works will never lead to salvation. To have your works or compliance with laws lead to salvation would be legalism or moralism. Only through faith in Christ can we be saved. He died to cover our sins; thus, we are no longer a slave to the law, no longer a slave to fear, and no longer a slave to sin. He freed us.

This is what Paul is telling the church. Salvation comes only through Jesus Christ, and the only thing that counts is faith in Christ expressing itself as love, not the law (Gal. 5:6). However, with this freedom comes responsibility. Paul is warning them not to again become a slave to the law or sin. Just because we have the grace and mercy available to us every day from Jesus Christ does not give us license to go around and sin and lead a life that would be displeasing to Jesus. We are to live a life of love. A life where the Holy Spirit works within us, through us, and in our communities. We are to use our freedom to serve one another humbly in love rather than indulge in the flesh (Gal. 5:13).

So, how do we walk by the Holy Spirit and love our neighbors? What does that look like? When you walk with the Spirit, your life produces the fruits of the Spirit; love, joy, peace, patience, kindness, goodness, faithfulness, gentleness, and self-control (Gal. 5:22–23). However, if you are not walking with the Spirit and are instead walking in self-indulgence then what you are producing is; sexual immorality, impurity, debauchery, idolatry, witchcraft, hatred, discord, jealousy, fits of rage, selfish ambition, dissension, factions, envy, drunkenness, orgies, and the like (Gal. 5:19–21). It is important to ask for the Holy Spirit to enter you, to be baptized by the Spirit water to live a life with the Spirit.

What Paul gives the church in chapter 5 of Galatians is the purpose of freedom. Too often in our culture today, we think about what freedom means for us. Paul is reminds us that freedom is given to us through Christ; however, the result is not self-indulgence or license to do whatever we want. The result ***should be*** a life of love toward others. If we want to feel the **freedom** Christ intended for us when He gave himself on the cross, then we need to open ourselves up to the Holy Spirit and let the love of Christ flow through us to those around us, and the fruits of the Spirit will be the evidence of the change Christ made in us!

The Struggle Within

"I have told you all this so that you may have peace in me. Here on earth you will have many trials and sorrows. But take heart, because I have overcome the world."

John 16:33 (NLT)

PRAYER

Father, evil is all around, and the world is dark, I need your light. Fill me with your Holy Spirit. Give me hope through the despair and struggles of this life. Strengthen me as I stumble, help me trust you with the decisions I have to make. Be my guide Lord. Help me find peace in your presence and to live my life in your will not my own. Thank you for your mercy and grace and your strength to help me through each day. Amen.

SONG

"Here Again"
by Elevation Worship

How Long Will You Run?

Many of us will feel a call that God puts in our hearts. That call could be to pastor a church, help the homeless, take care of the sick, or do mission work around the world. The point is that each of us will be a little different, but the source is the same. God wants to use us to further His Kingdom, but we have the choice to make; will we listen to that call or ignore it. That is not always an easy choice, as our human nature sometimes overrides our desire to serve our calling. The perfect example of this struggle can be seen in the life of the prophet Jonah.

Jonah is among the most famous of the prophets, not for what he prophesied, but for the extent he went to avoid the calling of God. As well as the extent God went to bring Jonah back. After all, God did have a large fish swallow Jonah and spat him back out where God wanted him to be. So, what can we learn from the prophet who ran?

We first learn that even if you run, it does not mean the calling will go away. Jonah was called to deliver a message to Nineveh, who was wicked and Jonah despised its people.

Jonah did not want to do it, so he ran, bought a ticket, and hopped on a boat to get as far away as he could (Jonah 1:1–3). God raised a violent storm on the sea, and the boat was in danger of being destroyed, but Jonah did not pray to God to stop it. Even when the non-believing sailors asked Jonah to pray to his God, Jonah only admitted it was his fault, and they needed to throw him overboard to stop the storm, and they did, and the storm stopped. All the sailors started serving God at that moment when they saw His power (1:4–16).

Jonah expected to die at this point and may have even hoped for death. He was running from God, he had seen God's anger as a result, but he still did not want to follow God's call. Once again, God had other plans for Jonah and had him swallowed by a large fish. Jonah spent three days and three nights inside that fish, and then he prayed (1:17). Did you catch that? Jonah did not pray on the boat in the storm or in the fish for three days! He was still running, but eventually he knew only God could deliver him, so he prayed.

The next thing Jonah shows us is the need for a repentant heart. God has a calling for your life; if you understand that calling and yet run from it, you will eventually need to ask God for his forgiveness. Jonah does this in his prayer. He remembers all the things God has done for him and how God saved him over and over, and even while in the belly of the fish he offered praise and promised to uphold his vows and calling. It was after this heartfelt repentance that God had the fish spit him out (2:1–10)

Jonah still fought his calling, yet God used him to deliver his message. The question, for all of us, is how long we will request God's calling in our life, and how much will we require God to keep dropping us back on the path? If you have felt a call on your life, then learn from the lessons God taught Jonah.

The calling will never go away because God will not go away. Repent and offer your praise to God to get back on the path God wants you on. Finally, walk the path. God will call others if you don't answer, but He is looking for your obedience and wants to use YOU! He chose you for a purpose, He created you for a purpose. Stop running, it's time to answer the call.

I Am Not Qualified to Be Used By God

Exodus 3, Philippians 4:13

Have you ever wondered why God would ever choose you to do anything for Him? I know that thought has crossed my mind for a time or two. There is someone more qualified I am; why did he not choose them? What we come to learn from the Bible is that this is a common practice for God. He often chooses people that would be unexpected and unqualified. The good news for us is that God does not call the qualified, he qualifies the called. There are so many great examples of this throughout the Bible, including one of the most famous Bible legends, Moses.

After his birth, Moses's mom put Moses in a basket and floated him down the river toward Pharoah's daughter. She saved and raised Moses as an Egyptian. However, he had to flee Egypt because he killed an Egyptian who was beating a Hebrew man. Moses ran so he himself would not be killed. Eventually, he ended up in Midian, where he married and settled down to live as a shepherd. He was living a quiet life until God called him. Exodus chapter 3 is where this story picks up. This is where God speaks to Moses from a burning bush. God calls him to lead Israel out of slavery.

When you read this passage, think about how crazy it would be to see a bush on fire, but it was not burning. Not just that, but then it starts talking to you! For us, it would be like walking through the living room, and the TV turns on while it is unplugged. Next, God starts speaking to you directly through the TV, using your name and everything! How crazy would that be? Moses must have been in shock and awe.

We have all asked at different times for God to drop a neon sign to tell us what to do, well here it is, Moses's neon sign. Surely a sign from God this obvious would make anyone follow what God asked. Plus, Moses is a hero of the Bible, so he must not have hesitated at all, or did he? As we read about Moses's response, we can see his doubt, not of God, but of himself. He did not follow God's calling immediately; he questioned if God had the right guy. Even Moses, a hero of the Bible, felt unqualified to do God's work, to be called by God.

Why would we be any different? But the truth is if God calls you, then you are ready, if you lean on God for your strength. That is why God uses everyday people because without Him, they could not accomplish what He asks. But with God, you can accomplish anything.

"For I can do everything through Christ, who gives me strength" Philippians 4:13.

God has great plans for you, even when or if you feel unqualified to be called. While God's calling likely will not appear in the form of a burning bush, understand He CHOSE YOU. Even though you are not perfect, He wants to use you. He knows you can do what He asks. If God believes in you, then you can believe in yourself because He will be with you. Just like Moses. In Moses, God raised a man who feared speaking in public and did not want to be God's voice to Pharaoh in leading Israel to the promised land.

Will there be moments of doubt? Sure. But God would never ask something of you that you could not do. So, what is causing your doubt right now? Do you know that God is with you? God is waiting for you to talk to Him about your doubt. Did God turn away Moses because of his doubt? No! He did not! And God will not turn from you, so bring it all to Him and know that He will listen and guide you. He will qualify the called.

Does Control Have a Hold on You?

John 11:45-53

One of the hardest things for all of us to let go of is control. For some, it is easy, but for most of us, it is hard. The desire for control or the desire to maintain control can cause us to sin in many ways. Pride is often at the root of this sin issue, and the belief that no one can do it better than we can. The irony is as believers in Christ, we are called to give up control. When you decide to follow Christ, accept His grace, and be saved, you are turning your life over to Him. He leads your life as you move from salvation to sanctification. So, at its foundation, faith is not just belief but a forfeit of control.

The reading for today focuses on when the desire to maintain control becomes so great that it leads to decisions that you would never consider in a moment of clarity. Specifically, the passage for this devotional focuses on the moment when the Pharisees decided they were going to kill Jesus. This takes place right after Jesus raises Lazarus from the dead.

When Jesus performed this miracle of raising a man from the dead, a man who had been dead for four days, many saw and believed that indeed Jesus was the long-awaited

Messiah. Could you imagine what it would have been like to be at the tomb when Lazarus came out? You knew he died four days ago, yet now he is walking right in front of you! The awe, the joy, and the love for your friend being back would be overwhelming. Would it not? However, in verse 46, we see that some, instead of believing and celebrating, went to the Pharisees and told them about what Jesus had done.

The Pharisees were the religious leaders of the day. Jesus was Jewish. The Jewish people were awaiting the coming Messiah, and now Jesus was performing miracles that would demonstrate He was the Messiah. As religious leaders, what must they have thought about what they were being told? Did they ask how Jesus had done this? Did they think about the joy that the family and friends of this man must surely be experiencing at this moment? Nope. None of that. What they thought and then decided, was they needed to kill Jesus.

They were not concerned that Jesus might be the Messiah they had been waiting for. They were not concerned that the power of God was on display through Jesus. What we see clearly in verse 48 is their concern was solely on the loss of their own power and control, if Jesus was allowed to continue showing these signs and wonders. "If we allow him to go on like this, soon everyone will believe in him. Then the Roman army will come and destroy both our Temple and our nation." We learn from the response of the Pharisees that the willingness to give up control is not only difficult, but the power of keeping control can tempt us to a point we cannot or will not overcome. For the Pharisees that desire for control led to them denying their faith, religion, and the very Messiah they had been waiting for over a thousand years to arrive. Then they took it a step further, and instead of just denying Jesus, they decided to kill Jesus. Talk about a poor decision.

So, how do we overcome the power of having control? No one is perfect in this area but the more you surrender your life to Christ, the more His blessings and miracles will move your heart instead of hardening it. Remember the foundation of faith is not just belief but also relinquishing control of your life to Jesus Christ. Let Him lead, and you will be amazed at the change He will create in you.

Self-Preservation vs. Blessed Assurance

John 18

Do you ever feel that publicly admitting you are a Christian, a believer in Jesus Christ, is potentially harmful to your reputation or even dangerous? Do you worry that speaking about Christ at work can get you in trouble? Do you feel that it is best to keep your belief to yourself because the perception of Christians in the world is not a positive one? Well, you are not alone.

Jesus had twelve disciples that traveled with Him during His ministry. Perhaps the most well know of the twelve was Peter. He was fiery, assertive, confident, strong and a leader. He was among the first to proclaim Jesus was the Son of God, the Messiah. He was ready to fight and die for the Kingdom and Jesus Christ. In fact, when the Romans came to take Jesus away to be tried, Peter cut off the ear of one of the soldiers coming to take Jesus (John 18:9). So, it seems unlikely that Peter himself would have ever had these feelings of self-preservation or protecting his reputation by not speaking of his friendship with Christ, or his belief in Him as the Messiah, but that is exactly what happens.

When Jesus is taken away, the disciples scatter. They are in fear for their lives, but Peter follows at a distance as does one other disciple that is unnamed (John 18:15). Peter has been told by Jesus that he will deny knowing Jesus three times that night, and the first of these occur in verse sixteen. By the time the rooster crows in the morning, Peter, the one who attacked the soldiers who came for Jesus with a sword, denied even knowing Him. Peter was in self-preservation mode. Peter was almost assuredly under attack from the demons of fear and anxiety, and he allowed them to win this battle. However, let us not focus on Peter's failure. We all fail at times. Let us focus on the other disciple that went into the inner court with Jesus that night.

What is interesting about this disciple is how little we know. We are not even given the name; we only know that he was known by the Sanhedrin and was allowed access to the inner court to watch the trial of Jesus. The way the other disciples ran and the fact that Peter denied even knowing Jesus, surely this disciple was ridiculed and arrested for being there and associated with Jesus. Nope. We hear nothing of what he went through. We hear nothing of his fear and anxiety that overwhelmed the other disciples and Peter. What was the difference? He was with Christ the whole time. His eyes were on Christ, not on fear, anxiety, or self-preservation. When he was alone in a room of men looking for a way to kill Jesus, he was not alone. Jesus was with him.

Sometimes one of the hardest things to do is talk about Jesus at work or with friends. We become filled with anxiety and fear. Will they think we are weird? Will they still be our friends? What if they do not believe? That fear stops us from taking an opportunity to share Jesus and potentially helping someone towards their salvation. What we need to remember is that feelings of fear, anxiety, or self-preservation are not from God. They are from the enemy trying to stop you from sharing. So, when you feel that way stop and pray. Pray in the name of Jesus and send those feelings back to where they came from. By sending them back in Jesus's name we are calling on His authority and placing our eyes on Christ! Do not be afraid of ever sharing Christ and admitting you love Him. Keep your eyes on Christ and all will be fine, our victory is in heaven not this world. Trust in Him; you will have blessed assurance and no worries about self-preservation.

If Christ Is With Us, Then How Is There Evil?

Matthew 13:24-30, 36-43

One of the most common misunderstandings Jesus had to explain to his listeners, and even his disciples revolved around the Kingdom of God being present. The Jewish people had an expectation of how the Messiah would come, and the way Jesus came to earth was not the picture they had in their minds. The anticipation was that the Messiah would come in like a warrior king and establish his Kingdom on earth, and in the process, get rid of all that were not His chosen people. Instead, Jesus came in as an infant. So, for much of his ministry, he needed to teach that the Kingdom of God was present. The problem that persisted then, and still today, was the problem of evil in the world. How could God be present in this world if evil was?

For thousands of years, this question has led to debates among scholars, theologians, pastors, and all other Christians. The study of this question is called a theodicy. So, is there an answer? And more importantly, what did Jesus have to say about this question since it was clearly an issue for the people he preached to? The short answer is no. Jesus did not give an answer expressly stating why evil exists, however he did give amazing insight into evil's presence in the world in his parable of the wheat and the weeds.

In this parable, a farmer plants wheat in a field, and overnight the enemy comes and sows weeds into the field. The problem is that the two are virtually indistinguishable from each other until they have grown big enough that their roots are entangled. Pulling the weeds at the point they are recognizable would kill the wheat. Harvesting them together would destroy the harvest because the weeds in question have poisonous seeds that would contaminate the flour. So, what is the solution? They had to be allowed to grow together until the time of harvest. At the time of harvest, the weeds would be separated out and burned, and the wheat would be bundled together and brought before the harvester to shine like the sun in the Father's Kingdom.

This parable teaches us three things. First, God permits the righteous and the wicked to coexist in the world. You may not even be able to tell them apart, until Christ returns. Secondly, the wicked will be separated out, judged, and destroyed. Third, the righteous will be gathered together, rewarded and brought into the presence of God.

As Jesus preached this parable to the audience, the question of why evil exists is not answered, but remember what Jesus is trying to help his audience understand. The Kingdom of God is present. It was present then and it is present today. Evil is also present, and the enemy is constantly sowing weeds among the wheat in this world in an attempt to win the world. However, Jesus claimed the victory on the cross, and evil will be separated out and destroyed at the second coming of Christ.

What we need to remember today is that the kingdom is present due to the ministry of Jesus and the work of the Holy Spirit, even though evil is present also. The presence of evil is not evidence that the kingdom is not at work and in the end, evil will be judged. Jesus is preaching patience and for believers to expect continued attacks from those who do not accept Jesus as Savior. This parable also provides a warning to change our behavior because judgment will happen, but it is also giving encouragement for a future blessing for all who believe, a blessing that will happen in the presence of the Father.

Prayer

"Do not be anxious about anything, but in every situation, by prayer and petition, with thanksgiving, present your requests to God. And the peace of God, which transcends all understanding will guard your hearts and your minds in Christ Jesus."

Philippians 4:6–7 (NIV)

·········· *PRAYER* ··········

Heavenly Father, I come before you today and give You all honor and praise. Worthles are you Lord for all praise. God, please strengthen my prayer life. Help me to be more consistent in my time with you in prayer. Prompt me when I am doing mindless things to instead spend that time with you in prayer. Help me to know who I truly am in Christ. Help me to know your Word so I can pray it. Help me to write down my own needs and the needs of others so that I can bring them to you in prayer. Make my life a prayer to you Lord. Amen

SONG

."Make My Life a Prayer to You".
by Keith Green

Teach Us to Pray, Lord

Matthew 6:9-13, Philippians 4:6

When God created man and woman in the garden, He had a special relationship with them. God would come down to the garden towalk and talk with Adam and Eve. God's intention was always for there to be a conversational, familial relationship between Himself and His creation. When Adam and Eve sinned among the many punishments was banishment from the garden, separation from God, and an end to their walking alongside Him in the physical realm. However, there was still prayer. Prayer is the way through which we can have our conversational, familial relationship with the Father. He desires it, and we are blessed to still talk with Jesus.

As we think about our own prayer life, there are certainly moments we wish it could be better, or maybe we find it just altogether boring. We do not feel a connection to God. We do not know what to say. We feel we are not good at prayer, and sometimes we even fall asleep while doing it. Far too many times, or perhaps every time, it has felt more like a monologue than conversation. What are we doing wrong? How can we make our prayer life come to LIFE? That is a question that many have struggled with throughout history. In fact, even the twelve disciples were unsure of how to pray, but they had the ultimate expert teacher. They had Jesus Christ to teach them how to pray.

In Luke 11:1, they asked Jesus, ". . . Lord, teach us to pray . . ." What followed in Luke 11:2–4 is what has become known as the Lord's prayer. This is also found in Matthew 6:9–13. "This then is how you should pray: 'Our Father in heaven hallowed be your name, your kingdom come, your will be done, on earth as it is in heaven. Give us today our daily bread. And forgive us our debts, as we also have forgiven our debtors. And lead us not into temptation, but deliver us from the evil one'"

Jesus begins by declaring God's holy (hallowed) name, praising His holiness. He then calls for God's kingdom to come to earth, for God to reign on earth and for God's will to be done, not our own. Jesus then asks for God's provision every day. Did you know that bread still has the meaning of provision today? Have you ever been asked if you are the bread winner of the household? God is the provider (Jehovah Jireh), and we should ask every day for His provision to get us through. Next, we repent and ask for forgiveness and the ability to extend that same forgiveness to those who have wronged us. Finally, we ask for protection from the enemy and deliverance from the enemy.

There are many points to this short prayer, but did you notice that they are all related to the power, grace, provision, and mercy of God the Father? God does want us to bring our petitions to Him, it tells us this in Phil. 4:6, (NIV) ". . . in every situation, by prayer and petition, with thanksgiving, present your request to God." However, to have a conversation with the Lord, we also need to praise him, recognize his holiness, and allow for moments of silence for him to speak to us instead of just praying a list of wants and needs. God desires to answer us, we just need to desire to speak with Him and not just to Him.

If we desire a more personal relationship with Jesus, it starts with prayer and the best part is that Jesus gives us direction on how we can pray. While this is not the only prayer or the only way to pray, how could we go wrong putting this prayer into our lives daily? Change the words to fit the conversational mode of today if you need to but keep the sentiment. God desires to be in a conversational, familial relationship with you. So, let us Pray!

Paul's Prayer of Thanksgiving

Colossians 1:3-14

One of my favorite discoveries, as I read the Bible, are prayers from the heroes of the Bible. When you can sit and read a prayer from Moses, David, Abraham, or Paul the connection is amazing. You see a template of how prayers from thousands of years ago were lifted to God and how those prayers are just as relevant today as they were then. The God we worship is the same yesterday, today, and forever and as his children whether you were living in the first century or in the twenty first century, He hears our prayers. However, praying can be one of the hardest things for some of us, especially when we lack confidence in our ability to pray. So, the Bible becomes a great place to give us direction and examples of how to pray. One of the topics of another devotional discusses the fact that even the disciples were unsure how to pray, so they asked Jesus to teach them. From that passage Jesus gave us what is now known as the Lord's prayer. So, how can there be a better prayer than what Jesus himself prayed? So, whenever you struggle to connect to your prayer life, we can look simply to the Lord's prayer and start praying the Lord's prayer.

The more you can connect to prayer and to your Savior, the more you find prayer entering into every part of your life, and that is what we see in Paul's prayer to the church at Colosse.

Paul wrote many of the books of the New Testament. These were written letters to churches, and at the start of each letter we often see a prayer. He lifts a prayer to God before he teaches the lessons God has given him to share. This is an important point for those of us that are striving to live a life that is more like Christ in all we do. Everything begins with prayer, sometimes it is a prayer of need, a prayer to prepare our hearts, and sometimes it is a prayer of thanksgiving for those in our lives. This is what we see in Paul's letter to the church in Colosse, and it is a great template for how we can offer prayers of thanksgiving for those we are walking with in Christ.

"We are writing to God's holy people in the city of Colosse, who are faithful brothers and sisters in Christ. May God our Father give you grace and peace. We always pray for you, and we give thanks to God, the Father of our Lord Jesus Christ. For we have heard of your faith in Christ Jesus and your love for all of God's people. . . You learned about the Good News from Epaphras . . . He has told us about your love for others that the Holy Spirit has given you" (1:2–8).

"So we have not stopped praying for you since we first heard about you. We ask God to give you complete knowledge of his will and to give you spiritual wisdom and understanding. The way you live will always honor and please the Lord, and your lives will produce every kind of good fruit. All the while, you will grow as you learn to know God better and better. We also pray that you will be strengthened with all his glorious power so you will have all the endurance and patience you need. May you be filled with joy, always thanking the Father" (1:9–12)

Notice how Paul first thanks God for those who are following Jesus Christ, but he doesn't stop there, he asks God to strengthen them and bless them even more so they can continue to do God's work. Take today to pray for those in your life that have blessed you. Use Paul's prayer as an example, give thanks for them and pray that God will continue to strengthen and bless them even more.

A Powerful Prayer

1 Chronicles 4:9-10

There are many prayers throughout the Bible. In fact, the book of Psalms is full of songs and prayers of rejoicing, lament, cries for help, prayers of thanksgiving and lots more. The Lord's prayer in Matthew 6:9–13 is a way to pray taught to us by Jesus himself. Many other prayers stand out in the Bible as well, but there is one prayer that shows up out of nowhere and when that happens, it is important to take notice. This prayer is from a man named Jabez, and it has much to teach us.

One of the reasons this prayer seems so unique is due to where it is placed in the Bible. It comes during a long list of some of the descendants of Judah. During this list what we are learning is who were the sons of Judah, and who were their sons and so on, until we come to 1 Chronicles 4:9–10. Here there is a break to tell us about Jabez, and these two verses are all that is ever mentioned about Jabez in the entire Bible.

"There was a man named Jabez who was more honorable than any of his brothers. His mother named him Jabez because his birth had been so painful. He was the one who prayed to the God of Israel, 'Oh, that you would bless me and expand my territory! Please be with me in all that I do, and keep me from all trouble and pain!' And God granted him his request." (1 Chron. 4:9–10)

Did you catch the meaning of his name? His name was chosen to be a constant reminder of the pain he had caused. How must it have felt for Jabez to be reminded every time someone mentioned his name that he caused his mother great pain? Yet still, living under this cloud of negativity, Jabez reached out for the light of God, and in this prayer there is so much we can learn for our own prayer lives.

The prayer of Jabez has four parts that give us insight into what makes this prayer so powerful and why it needs to be included in the Bible. First, Jabez starts by asking for a blessing from God. "Oh, that you would bless me." God desires to bless his children, yet so many times we go right into our prayers asking about our needs, when the first need we have is to be blessed by God. Jabez knew the power of being blessed by God, and the desire of God to bless us.

Second, Jabez asked for God to "expand his territory." Many have discussed this as a prosperity gospel, just ask God to give you everything you desire, and he will because you believe in Him. But, what Jabez is asking for is an expansion of influence, of his ability to share God further. Remember, Jabez was more honorable than all his brothers, he would not have been asking for wealth, he wanted to share more of God.

Third, he fully surrenders to God. "Please be with me in all that I do." He is not offering God part of his life; he wants God in ALL his life. In EVERY step. Finally, he asks for God's protection. "Keep me from trouble and pain." He knows that the prayer he is praying is powerful, and the enemy will attack. Protection that comes from the spiritual armor of God is not only available but necessary.

This was not a prayer of selfishness; it was a prayer of selflessness. Jabez wanted more for God, not for himself. Do you want to pray powerful prayers? Here is a template. Ask for the blessing of Jesus, ask Him to give you more opportunities to share Him, surrender fully every part of your life and day to Jesus, and ask Him to protect you with the armor of God as you move forward reaching others for the glory of God.

When God's Answer to Your Prayer is No

2 Samuel 12, 2 Corinthians 12, Luke 22:42

The Bible is full of amazing answers to prayer and awesome displays of God's miraculous power. Moses prayed and God parted the Red Sea. Elijah prayed and called down fire from God. Daniel, alone in a lion's den, prayed and God shut the mouths of the lions. Shadrach, Meshach, and Abednego prayed, and God saved them in the fiery furnace. So, why are some of my prayers not answered when they seem so much less than these displays of power and wonder? You are not alone. Even some of the great heroes of the Bible prayed and God answered "no."

King David, a man after God's own heart, in 2 Samuel 12 receives a devastating "no" to his prayer. After David committed adultery with Bathsheba and had her husband Uriah killed to cover it up, they had a baby. Soon that baby became deathly ill. David prays and fasts for the healing of his son. Praying so hard that for seven days he cannot even stand without help, but the son still dies. Upon hearing this, what does David do? He cleans himself up, eats some food and goes to worship God. When asked why he responded the way he did, David gave some powerful insight into faith and prayer. "David replied, 'I fasted and wept while the child was alive', for I said, 'Perhaps the LORD will be gracious to me and let the child live.' But why should I fast when he is dead? Can I bring him back again? I will go to him one day, but he cannot return to me" (2 Sam. 12:22–23). David understood the power of prayer, that God could heal his son. God would heal his son, but it would not be immediately, or eventually, it would be eternally.

David wanted it immediately, but God said no. David found comfort in knowing that He would eventually see his son again because the healing was eternal. Paul experienced a "no" to his prayer also. A "thorn" was placed in his side, and he prayed three times for God to remove it, but the answer was no. God used this "thorn" to help Paul understand the reliance on God, that in our weakness, God's power is made perfect. (2 Cor. 12:7–9). In each "no," there were lessons to learn. However, the greatest "no" ever given to a prayer was the "no" given to Jesus.

When Jesus prayed in the garden before his arrest and eventual crucifixion, he asked God if there was another way, a different path. "Father, if you are willing, please take this cup of suffering away from me. Yet I want your will to be done, not mine" (Luke 22:42). What a difference it would have been for all of us if God would have said "Yes." Instead, God said "no," and Christ went to the cross willingly and died for all our sins, and now we have a path towards forgiveness, a relationship with God, and eternity with Him. All because God answered Jesus's prayer with "no."

It can be frustrating when God does not answer our prayer, but we can have faith that there is a purpose behind the no, one we may not understand until Heaven. David, Paul, and even Jesus experienced a "no" to their prayer, so you are not alone. It does not mean you lack the faith necessary for a yes. It just means God has a bigger plan that you cannot see but you can trust that He is working. And, because of the "no" God gave to Jesus, there is now one prayer that the answer will always be "Yes." That prayer is when you come to Jesus and truly ask for forgiveness, and for Jesus to be your Savior. For that prayer, Jesus will always answer "YES!"

Grace/Love/Salvation

"But God proves his own love for us in that while we
were still sinners, Christ died for us. How much more then,
since we have now been justified by his blood,
will we be saved through him from wrath."

Romans 5:8–9 (CSB)

PRAYER

Dear Lord, help me never forget all you do for me every day. You provide me with countless blessings, you are always with me, you will never leave nor forsake me, and you sustain me with your promise of salvation through the blood of Jesus Christ. Lead me, Lord, to live a life that is a testimony to you. A life that shares your light into this world, speaks of your incredible blessings and love, and saving grace available for all your children. May your love be known and experienced by all those I serve and come into contact with every day. In Jesus name. Amen.

SONG

........"Seat at the Table".......
by iTown Worship

The Renewing Power of God

Acts 16:25, Isaiah 40:31, Psalm 73:26, Joshua 1:9

It is amazing, some may even say crazy, how being in the presence of God can completely change your mood, attitude, and even your outlook in life in an instant. Whether you enter God's presence through a worship song, a moment of prayer, or a specific verse that speaks to you, God can take you from having the worst mindset to a place of peace and joy. We may enter his presence on our own or in a gathering of believers, but each time there is an opportunity for renewal. The Bible demonstrates this through examples of renewal of those in the Bible and in direct verses that speak to God's renewing power.

One of the apostle Paul's many astonishing stories takes place in prison. In this story, Paul and Silas have been arrested and beaten severely because they were preaching the gospel. Surely, at this point, even though they were suffering for the cause of Christ, they had to be feeling a little down in the spirit at this time. Prison is not the place anyone wants to be. So, what did they do to renew their strength and spirit? "Around midnight, Paul and Silas were praying and singing hymns to God, and the other prisoners were listening" (Acts 16:25). They prayed and sang worship songs! God shook the prison that night to the point the jail doors swung open. He may not cause a literal shake in your surroundings, but He will shake the prisons of fear and anxiety that the enemy has used to surround you.

The Bible assures us that God is there to renew us, that He is our strength. "My flesh and my heart may fail, but God is the strength of my heart and my portion forever" (Psalm 73:26, NIV). God will renew our strength if we put our hope in Him. "But those who hope in the Lord will renew their strength. They will soar on wings like eagles; they will run and not grow weary; they will walk and not be faint" (Isa. 40:31, NIV).

Perhaps another passage that sums up the impact of the power of God on renewing peace and joy in our lives was sung by King David in Psalm 23. "The Lord is my shepherd; I have all that I need. He lets me rest in green meadows he leads me beside peaceful streams. He **renews** my strength. He guides me along the right paths, bringing honor to his name. Even when I walk through the darkest valley, I will not be afraid, for you are close beside me. Your rod and your staff protect and comfort me. You prepare a feast for me in the presence of my enemies. You honor me by anointing my head with oil. My cup overflows with blessings. Surely your goodness and unfailing love will pursue me all the days of my life, and I will live in the house of the Lord forever" (Psalm 23).

David saw the hope in following God, in letting God shepherd him through life. He saw the renewing of his strength even when he was in the darkest times of his life. He saw this because he looked to God as his protector and provider, and God gave him peace in those moments and poured his blessings out as David entered His presence. God can do the same for you because you are never alone when you have God.

"Do not be afraid or discouraged. For the Lord your God is with you wherever you go" (Josh. 1:9). We need to make the time to enter his presence in song, prayer, or reading the Bible to feel the renewing power of God and the peace and joy that can come in an instant. And we do not have to wait until our darkest hour to do so. We can come to him every day, throughout the day for his renewing power and love! Plug in for His renewing power!

Dead Bones Come to Life

Ezekiel 37:1-28

How do you know you can always have hope when you have God? At times, maybe even as you are reading this, you may feel that all hope is gone. You feel or have felt that there is nothing that can be done to save you. Even God is powerless to overcome the void and emptiness that your life is currently experiencing. While that may seem like reality, the truth is there is always hope when God is involved.

One of the more interesting passages in the Bible comes in the book of Ezekiel. The passage concerns Ezekiel's vision of a valley filled with dry, bleached bones (37:1–2). These people had died long ago and had been left unburied. They may have been soldiers that fell in battle, but whatever the situation, they were clearly long gone and well past life. This was a fitting description of Israel at the time. They were hopeless, in exile, defeated, and devoid of the joy of a life with God. Could anything possibly be done to free Israel from this despair? Can anything be done for you? Yes, and Yes. When God is involved, there is always hope.

As the vision unfolds God tells Ezekiel to speak to the bones and tell them, "I will make breath enter you, and you will come to life" (37:5, NIV). As Ezekiel spoke over the bones, they began to form back into human form but there was still no life in them. "Then he said to me, 'Prophesy to the breath; prophesy, son of man, as say to it, 'This is what the Sovereign LORD says: Come, breath, from the four winds and breathe into these slain, that they may live.'' So I prophesied as he commanded me, and breath entered them; they came to life and stood up on their feet—a vast army" (37:9–10, NIV). When the breath came into them the bones came alive! The point of this for Israel, Ezekiel, and all of us reading it today is that these people were really, really dead, yet with God, they were brought back to life. Where all hope seemed gone, with God, the impossible was possible. With God, hope was not lost, it was reality! The key was the breath of God entering into the bones in verses 9–10.

The Hebrew word used here is Ruah, referring to breath. It is literally the breath of God, the infilling of the Spirit of God, that breathed life into the bones. The word Ruah is used 389 times in the Hebrew scriptures, but in this chapter of Ezekiel, it is used 10 times, so it is important to the passage. What stands out the most is that while the army seemed to be alive, having taken on human form, it was not until the breath of God was breathed into them that they were truly alive. So, Israel may seem to exist by outward appearance, and a person may seem to exist by outward appearance as well, but until the Lord breaths into you His Spirit or puts His Spirit within you, there is no true life.

If you are at that point in your life where you have no hope, where God does not seem near or to care, then it is time to pray. Pray for the Spirit of God, the Ruah, to enter you. If God can restore dry bones to life, and restore a fallen Israel repeatedly, He can bring anyone else back to life that He chooses.

You do not have to live a life without hope because when you are with God there is always hope. The key is you need to call on Him, submit to Him, and surrender your life to Him. Trust in the Lord. Nowhere in Ezekiel 37 did Ezekiel do anything that caused life. All Ezekiel did was trust and follow the directions of the Lord, and God's breath, His Ruah brought life.

A Portrait of Grace

Jesus Christ changed the world forever when He went to the cross to suffer and die for my sins and your sins. He was perfect and had never sinned, but Jesus still stepped into our place to take the punishment for our sins to bring us back into a relationship with God. This is what is meant by the grace of God. It is the undeserved favor of God, demonstrated by our salvation through Jesus Christ and the blessings that God gives us. The word grace is mentioned in the New Testament over one hundred times and is central to the core beliefs of Christianity, and the gift of being reconciled to God. However, one of the best portraits of grace in the Bible comes to us in the Old Testament. This is in the story of King David and the grandson of King Saul, Mephibosheth. Through this story we as believers can have a portrait of the grace God had for us when we were sinners, and He chose not death but saved us through grace.

When King Saul died, it set the stage for the anointed King David to finally ascend to the throne of Israel. For many of the years leading up to this, Saul had been trying to kill David to keep him from the throne, but now David was King. It was common, at this time for the incoming king to kill any of the remaining sons or grandsons of the previous king to prevent them from seeking the crown, and this is where the story of Mephibosheth begins. He was about 5 years old when his grandfather and father died. When his nurse heard of their deaths, she fled with him and as she was fleeing, he fell and became crippled in both feet, but he lived and moved far away (2 Sam. 4:4).

Years later, David desires to show kindness to the house of Saul for the sake of his closest friend Jonathan, who was Mephibosheth's father. So, he asks if there is anyone still living that he can show kindness to (2 Sam. 9:1). He is told of Mephibosheth and had him brought from far away to him. Surely, Mephibosheth would have considered this a death sentence as all his family was dead, but death was not what David had planned. Instead, he planned grace!

Mephibosheth arrives and falls on his face in front of David and exclaims that he is useless and should not even be considered by the King as anything more (9:6–8). However, David changes everything in an instant. In honor of his best friend Jonathan, David decides to show grace and restores all of Saul's lands to his grandson. Mephibosheth also is invited to eat at his table for the rest of his life. David could have ended his life and ignored him as useless, but instead, he restored him and gave him a seat at his table.

We come to Jesus broken and useless, just as Mephibosheth came to David. For our sins we should be punished and die. The Bible says, "for the wages of sin is death" (Rom. 6:23). Instead, we are offered the gift of grace and salvation, "but

the free gift of God is eternal life through Christ Jesus our Lord" (Rom. 6:23). David gives the gift of grace to Mephibosheth, and not only spares his life, but gives him a seat at his royal table. We come broken to the feet of Jesus, and when we surrender to Him, we are given the gift of grace. We are SAVED and have been given a seat at His table (Luke 14). David offers us a portrait of grace hundreds of years before Jesus Christ offered up not just a portrait of grace but true grace! Your seat is waiting. Are you ready?

How Much Does Jesus Love You?

Matthew 8:1-3, John 3:16

One of the most quoted verses of the Bible is John 3:16 "For God so loved the world that He gave His one and only Son, that whoever believes in Him shall not perish but have eternal life." This verse speaks to the Father's love for us and the love Jesus has for us. God sent Jesus to earth to die for our sins, although he himself did nothing to deserve that fate. Jesus accepted that punishment for you and me. He stepped into the gap that sin created between God and us and willingly died so that we could be with God again. So much in this verse speaks to the love God the Father and Christ the Son have for us, but for this devotional, we are going to focus on another passage that demonstrates Christ's unconditional love.

In Matthew 8:1–3 (NIV), Jesus heals a man with leprosy. "When Jesus came down from the mountainside, large crowds followed him. A man with leprosy came and knelt before him and said, 'Lord, if you are willing, you can make me clean.' Jesus reached out his hand and touched the man. 'I am willing,' he said, 'Be clean!' Immediately he was cleansed of his leprosy."

To understand the love Jesus demonstrates here, we first need to understand more about leprosy. Leprosy is an infectious disease that mainly causes skin lesions and nerve damage but can also lead to crippling deformities. Today there are treatments for leprosy, as it does still exist, but in the time of Jesus there was no known cure and as a result those labeled as lepers were in for a life of extreme hardship.

First and foremost, anyone with leprosy would have to move away from friends and family. Often, they would find themselves living in colonies outside of town with other lepers. The move was necessary due to the high level of contagiousness of the disease, however there was another spiritual reason that you were an outcast, as well. It was believed at the time that leprosy was a result of sinfulness in your life. Leprosy was God's way of punishing you for the wrong you had done. So, you were isolated from everyone you loved and discarded by everyone who loved you.

The hardship didn't stop there. When you were out in public you couldn't hide. It was your responsibility to make sure everyone around you knew you were a leper. To accomplish this, you were to yell "unclean" anytime someone was visible to you so that they knew to stay away. Your isolation became more and more pronounced.

Now, consider the leper in Matt. 8:1–3. He is clearly violating all the laws on how a leper should act in public. He is in the midst of a large crowd, and we are not told he is yelling "unclean." Instead, he is kneeling before Jesus and asking Jesus to touch him and heal him. When the crowd noticed him, they likely recoiled and scattered to get away, but not Jesus. He did not run, He did not turn away, and Jesus touched him! This was likely the first physical touch the leper had received in years, but Jesus didn't see a leper. Jesus, when he turned, saw a child he loved, and His love touched and healed this man. What a powerful demonstration of love! Where society isolated and separated Jesus reached out and touched!

Please know that there is nothing that would ever keep Jesus from reaching out to you. He will reach for you when no one else will, just like the leper. Every time! You will never be too dirty, too unworthy of his forgiveness. You can never earn His love, but do you know what is great? You don't have to! It is freely given to you and for you! All you need to do is reach out your hand, open your heart, and take hold! Say, "Jesus, make me clean."

The Room Where It Happens

Exodus 26, Exodus 30,
Leviticus 16, Matthew 27:50-51

One song from the hit Broadway musical Hamilton is the song, "The Room Where It Happens." In this song, Aaron Burr is lamenting that he is not in the room with the key decision makers making the decisions that will impact the young nation. It's reserved for a small few. A similar situation can be seen where the presence of God was located in the Old Testament. The Jewish people built a temple for God, the first one that could be moved, and eventually, a permanent structure. Within this temple, one room was called the Holy of Holies. Only the high priest was allowed into the room, and only on the Day of Atonement.

In Exodus 26:31–33 the building of the Holy of Holies is described, and we learn that what separates the Holy of Holies from the holy place is a large veil. Exodus 30:6 discusses the altar in front of the mercy seat in the Holy of Holies, the mercy seat is where the presence of God will rest. Later, in Leviticus 16, the instructions of who can enter are given. In Leviticus, only Aaron, the high priest, can enter, and only on the Day of Atonement. What happens if he enters at the wrong time? He will die. No one else can even be in the tent of meeting, let alone the Holy of Holies, while Aaron is meeting with God.

So, there are lot of rules that specify what can be done in the Holy of Holies, who can be there, when they can be there, and what happens if they go in when they are not supposed to go in. Surely many wanted to be in the room where it happens, where you meet with the presence of God. However it was reserved for only one, and only one day a year. It would stay that way for thousands of years, until one Friday, one Good Friday, everything changed.

On Good Friday, the day Christ was crucified, something amazing happened. We were all once again given an opportunity to have a path to God. We had been separated by our sin and unable to be in God's presence, but Christ changed everything. When he offered himself as atonement for our sins, he went to the mercy seat of God for that atonement, just like the high priests had done for the atonement of the sins of the people of Israel. When God accepted this atonement, Jesus died, and at that very moment everything changed.

Matthew 27:50–51 (NIV) "And when Jesus had cried out again in a loud voice, he gave up his spirit. At that moment, the curtain of the temple was torn from top to bottom."

With the supernatural tearing of the veil there is no longer a barrier between God and His people. We now have a direct path through the Holy of Holies because of the atoning sacrifice of Jesus Christ. The veil being torn into two signified this exact moment. The High Priest, Jesus Christ, entered the Holy of Holies, offered himself as the atoning sacrifice, and now we all get to be in the room where it happens. We can have that relationship in the room where God's presence is located, without needing an intermediary. We can come to the mercy seat because Christ tore the veil and gave us access again to a relationship with God the Father.

One supernatural event tore down a veil that had separated man from God for thousands of years, a veil that hid behind it the presence of God and the threat of death if entered when not allowed. Now death has removed that veil, and we are all given access to the room where it happens.

Parable of the Lost Sheep

Luke 15:1-7

Have you ever felt that you were not important? That there were so many others that were or are better than you? I can guarantee you that you are not alone. So, what do we do with the fact that Jesus knows each one of us? He died on the cross so that you and I can be saved. It is hard for that to make sense to any of us, but that is exactly what he did. Jesus often taught in parables, and at one point, He taught a parable that shows the love that the Father has for everyone. It is the parable of the lost sheep.

To set the scene for this parable, it is important to know to who Jesus was speaking as that was the purpose of the parable, to teach those who heard it. Jesus was at the time being chastised for allowing tax collectors and other notorious sinners to come and listen to him teach. The Pharisees and teachers of the religious law were angry that Jesus allowed this and that he was associating with this group of sinners. So, as Jesus taught this parable, it is important to understand that two audiences, the Pharisees and the sinners, were listening to Him that day. And for each, there would be a similar yet different message.

"So Jesus told them this story: 'If a man has a hundred sheep and one of them gets lost, what will he do? Won't he leave the ninety-nine others in the wilderness and go to search for the one that is lost until he finds it? And when he has found it, he will joyfully carry it home on his shoulders. When he arrives, he will call together his friends and neighbors, saying, 'Rejoice with me because I have found my lost sheep.' In the same way there is more joy in heaven over one lost sinner who repents and returns to God than over ninetynine others who are righteous and haven't strayed away!'" (Luke 15:3–7)

So, first let us look at what this would mean to the Pharisees and teachers of the law. They complained that Jesus was associating with and teaching sinners. They thought that teaching the Word of God should be reserved for only those that were "righteous." Jesus turns that notion completely on its head. In verse seven Jesus says, "there is more joy in heaven over one lost sinner that repents to God than over ninety-nine others who are righteous and haven't strayed away!" God is constantly looking for the lost to bring them home.

We must understand that God loves those who have not strayed just as much as he loves the sinner, but they are already with God. It is when the lost return and join the fold that heaven has a party (Luke 15:10). God is here for all the lost, not just those who are already saved. His love and Word are for everyone!

For the sinners in the crowd this teaching from the Messiah himself must have been overwhelming in the sense of finally belonging. Their whole lives, they were outcasts, they were cut off from associating with those that followed God, and they were not even allowed to dine with them. They were unwanted, unloved, and unworthy of the grace and mercy of God. Then Jesus spoke, and every negative thought they had about how God perceived them, or if He even cared, was turned upside down.

No matter where you are in life or what you have done, God is constantly seeking you out, desiring to bring you back into the fold. And when you finally surrender to God and ask Jesus into your heart, a party begins in Heaven where all are shouting YOUR NAME because the lost sheep has been found and is finally home!

Made in the Image of God

Genesis 1:27, Mark 12:13-17

It is not far into creation that humanity arrives on the scene, but right away, we are told there is something different about this part of creation. "So God created human beings in *his own image*. In the image of God he created them; male and female, he created them" (Gen. 1:27). This is far different than the rest of creation that God breathed into existence. Whether it is light, darkness, oceans, land, sun, moon, stars, or animals, none of them were created in the image of God! Only human beings were made in His image. So, why is that important?

Truthfully, I had never put much thought into being made in the image of God. I just thought it made sense because we are children of God, so we should reflect His image. After all, that is what it is like for our children. They usually reflect the image of their parents. However, as I was reading in the New Testament, I came across a passage in the Gospel of Mark that completely changed the way I now look at being made in the image of God.

In Mark 12, the Pharisees are trying to trap Jesus into saying something that could get him arrested. Paying taxes was a law then just as it is today, and not paying them could result in being arrested and sent to prison. So, they challenged Jesus, asking him in Mark 12:14–15, "Now tell us—is it right to pay taxes to Caeser or not? Should we pay them or shouldn't we?" Jesus saw the trap as they handed him a coin, and it is in his response that a whole new insight into being made into the image of God can be seen. "When they handed it to him (the coin), he asked, 'Whose picture and title are stamped on it?' 'Caeser's,' they replied. 'Well, then,' Jesus said, 'give to Caeser what belongs to Caeser, and give to God what belongs to God.' His reply completely amazed them" (Mark 12:16–17).

Because the coin carried Caesar's likeness and image, Christ said it belonged to Caeser. However, he finished the conversation by telling them to give to God what belongs to God. If we are made in the image of God, in the likeness of God, then does not that also mean we belong to God? How amazing is it to know that in Gen. 1:27, WE are made in the image of God in the likeness of God, and as a result, WE belong to God!

If you have ever felt forgotten by God, or are unimportant, then this verse should show you how important you are. You belong to God, and He will not forget that which belongs to Him. Thus, our commitment, devotion, love, loyalty, and service to our Father are all proper responses for those who bear his image and belong to Him.

So, the next time you read Gen. 1:27 I want you to think of being made in God's image! Not just as you being a reflection of God but as you belonging to God. Whatever your day, week, month, or year has been you can rest in knowing that you are beautifully and wonderfully made in our Father's very image! And not just that, but you also belong to our Father.

God knows your name. He has known it from the beginning of time. Your name, He knows it! And if there is ever an opportunity for someone to walk up to God and ask Him if he knows you, the answer would be a very clear. Yes. I know them. I know them because they belong to me. They are one of mine. Friends, you are not forgotten, ever. Your name has been on God's heart from the beginning of time.

Are You Ready?

"But in your hearts regard Christ the Lord as holy, ready at any time to give a defense to anyone who asks you for a reason for the hope that is in you."

1 Peter 3:15 (CSB)

PRAYER

Heavenly Father, as I begin another day, I ask you to help me to be ready for whatever comes my way. I pray for your will to be done Lord on earth as it is in heaven. If there is a need, then send me. If I am to stand, then give me the courage to do so. If I am to be still, then help me be filled with the peace that passes all understanding. If I am to do nothing, then help me wait patiently for your call. I ask for your Holy Spirit to fill me, to erase any doubt and indecision on my part so that I may walk with you along your path. I need your strength, your Spirit, your courage, your guidance and your wisdom Lord. Help me to be ready. Send me. Amen.

SONG

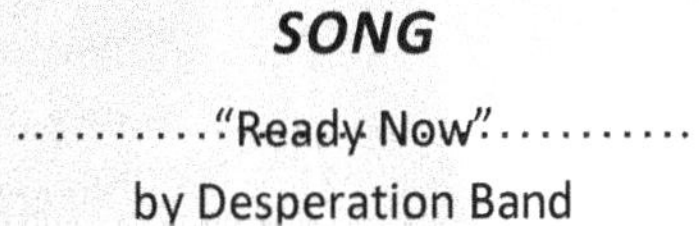

"Ready Now"
by Desperation Band

What is God Preparing You For?

Philippians 1:6, Genesis 5-9

Have you ever felt underqualified for something you were asked to do? Maybe you have felt if given time, you could get there, but not as quickly as you are being asked to deliver. Have you ever experienced a drought, where nothing seems to be moving forward, and there is little to no purpose in your day to day? Maybe you have felt a calling from God on your life, but nothing is happening, and nothing has been happening to move you toward that calling in a long, long time. Or have you prayed a specific prayer but now find yourself stuck in the waiting? Let me assure you of two things, you are not alone, and God is not done with you yet!

Phil. 1:4–6 (NIV) says, ". . . I always pray with joy . . . being confident of this, that he who began a good work in you will carry it on to completion until the day of Christ Jesus." Even in these times of waiting, these times of silence and quiet, these times of feeling underqualified for the role you are put in, there is a purpose. God is preparing you! Every one of us has been created by God with the ability to serve God and the Kingdom. We have each been called to something. Some will answer that call, others will not, but each call takes preparation. Unfortunately, preparation requires patience, a resource many of us lack.

An exceptional example of faith and patience in a time of preparation is given to us in Genesis, through the story of Noah. Most people know the story of Noah and the flood, but have you ever considered what it took Noah to get to that point? Have you considered how God used time to prepare Noah and build his faith? We know that Noah was about five hundred years old when God came to him and told him about the flood He would bring to destroy the earth (Gen 5:32). We know that when the flood ended, Noah was 601 (Gen 8:13), and he and his family had spent a year on the ark. Did you catch that? Noah spent one hundred years preparing for something that lasted 1 year!

There is no doubt that during the time of constructing the ark, Noah would have had moments of doubt, and his faith would have been tested. After all, Noah was not a boat builder; surely, neighbors thought he was crazy. It never even rained here, why build a boat? It is also unlikely that God spoke to Noah every day. If God told Noah it was going to flood, why was it taking so long? God could have supernaturally created the boat in a brief time or brought others to help. Instead, Noah had to rely on his faith and the promises of God to get him through the building of the ark. However, what God was preparing Noah for was not the flood, it was the 350 years after when Noah would lead the rebuilding of civilization.

Many of us have expectations that we take into our interactions with God. We believe we know what it should look like and how God should prepare us for what we feel called to. However only God truly knows the plan for our lives. This time of uncertainty, this time of waiting, this time of silence, and this time of feeling underqualified are all just trials of our faith and patience while God prepares us for something.

God told Noah to prepare for a flood, but what God was preparing Noah for during those one hundred years was what *would come*! He needed a man of faith to lead humanity, rebuild civilization, and rely on God's promises. God did not need an ark, he needed more! He needed Noah to prepare for one hundred years to be ready for that moment. So, in your waiting, you should ask, what is God preparing you for?

Parable of the Sower

Matthew 13:1-23

As you read the gospels of Matthew, Mark, Luke, and John, one thing that stands out is that Jesus often taught by using parables. A parable is just a simple story that is used to teach a lesson. So, when Jesus taught in parables there was a specific meaning and message he was trying to convey to those listening. At times there are multiple lessons in one parable depending on the number of characters in the story, and that is exactly what we see with the parable of the Sower.

Jesus lived in an agrarian society, so some of the parable characters will be unfamiliar to those of us who do not, but a Sower is simply the one who plants the crops that will be harvested. In Jesus's time, they clearly did this by hand.

"A farmer went out to sow his seed. As he was scattering the seed, some fell along the path, and the birds came and ate it up. Some fell on the rocky places, where it did not have much soil. It sprang up quickly, because the soil was shallow. But when the sun came up, the plants were scorched, and they withered because they had no root. Other seed fell among the thorns, which grew up and choked the plants. Still other seed fell on good soil, where it produced a crop—a hundred, sixty or thirty times what was sown. Whoever has ears let him hear." (Matt. 13:3–9, NIV)

Jesus was preaching this message to a large crowd, and as they listened, they would have understood that the seed was the gospel message, and the understanding that Jesus was the Messiah. Some would choose to believe and allow that seed to be planted in good soil, many would not, and their faith would not grow or would be choked out. Jesus explains this part to the disciples in verses 18–23. However, for these twelve men the parable had a second lesson to teach. The seed being planted was still the gospel message, however the disciples were going to have the role of the Sower in the parable. They were the ones that would be taking the gospel message to the world after Jesus.

Jesus knew the disciples had to understand the impact of the gospel on those who heard it, and he also needed the disciples to understand the importance of not being selective about where to preach but preaching to all. Often a Sower cannot tell where the seed will fall and if he slows down to plant in only what looks like good soil, he will never plant his whole field in time. He understands that for the best harvest, some seeds will fall where they will not grow.

As believers, we are called to share Jesus with everyone, this can be through leading someone to Christ, or it could be by letting Jesus shine through you with how you live your life. Sometimes that message will fall on fertile ground, other times, it will not, but we are to spread the message of Jesus everywhere.

It is never up to us to decide who should hear the message of God's mercy and grace and the love of Jesus Christ. We also cannot expect to force the decision of a person given free will to make a choice to believe. So, what can we do? We can make sure everyone has the same chance to be saved. Jesus said at the end of the parable, "Whoever has ears let him hear." So, just as it was for the disciples, we are the Sower, and the gospel is the seed. We are to share it with everyone through words or in how we live our life. We sow the seed and God will nurture and water it, and where it falls in good soil, it will produce a crop up to a hundred times what was sown!

A Leader Can Come from Anywhere

Have you ever felt that God has called you to a path that seems impossible for you to accomplish? Perhaps you believe you lack the authority or position needed to lead in the way to which you are called. Maybe you feel you are too young or not strong enough in your faith and confidence to lead. The prophet Jeremiah knew exactly how you feel, he was going through the same feelings when God called him to be the prophet to Israel.

Jeremiah was young, yet he was to be the voice of God to a nation. Scholars estimate that Jeremiah was thirteen to sixteen when God called him to begin his ministry. He was only a teenager! And he would be asked to deliver hard messages to Israel. How intimidating to tell priests and leaders they are turning from God, and the Bible tells us Jeremiah was scared.

"The word of the Lord came to me, saying, 'Before I formed you in the womb I knew you, before you were born, I set you apart, I appointed you as a prophet to the nations.' 'Alas, Sovereign Lord,' I said, 'I do not know how to speak;

I am too young.' But the Lord said to me, 'Do not say, 'I am too young.' You must go to everyone I send you to and say whatever I command you. Do not be afraid of them, for I am with you and will rescue you,' declared the Lord." (Jer. 1:4–8, NIV)

At his age, he clearly had no civil authority. How would he have the strength to deliver hard messages to the leaders of Israel? He would have put his trust in God and relied on God's strength to get him through. He needed God's strength when he told the priests that God was going to destroy Israel again if they did not turn back to God.

"Say to them, 'This is what the Lord says: If you do not listen to me and follow my law, which I have set before you, and if you do not listen to the words of my servants the prophets, whom I have sent to you again and again, then I will make this house like Shiloh and this city a curse among the nations of the earth.'" (Jer. 26:4–6, NIV).

As soon as Jeremiah delivered this message the priest grabbed Jeremiah and started yelling that he must die! He was brought before the officials in hopes of them rendering a death sentence, and in this moment the faith and trust in God that Jeremiah lived with shone through. He spoke God's message and told the leaders they must make the choice to follow, but they could do whatever they thought was right to him. However, they must understand that God's judgement was near. (Jer. 26:8–15)

Can you imagine how scary this must have been for Jeremiah? He was simply doing what God had called him to do and he was being threatened with death. Think about what you would feel in that situation or even imagine what you would say. Jeremiah shared the message and put his trust in God to protect him. He left everything up to God's will, not his own.

Trusting in God fully is hard. It means giving up our control and trusting in God's unseen plan, but when you surrender to His plan, you will truly feel peace. God may ask you to do what seems impossible, like Jeremiah. When God gives you a path that seems impossible, put your trust and faith in Him. God will bless you beyond what you can imagine. So, no matter your age, position, confidence, or authority, when God calls you to lead, know you can because God is with you!

The Roadmap for Happiness

Psalm 1:1-3, Luke 15:11-31

It is fair to say that most of us want many things out of life, but if we could find happiness, that would be among our greatest desires. As a result, we seek happiness in a variety of places. We look for it in friends, family, work, and hobbies to mention a few. However, we do not always consider the negative impact some of these can have on us or what to do when they have a negative impact. Fortunately, we have been given a roadmap to happiness in Psalm 1. It seems fitting that the first Psalm should center around this, as the Psalms lead us into praise, worship, prayer, lament, and exultation throughout the rest of the book.

"Oh, the joys of those who do not follow the advice of the wicked, or stand around with sinners, or join in with mockers. But they delight in the law of the Lord, meditating on it day and night. They are like trees planted along the riverbank, bearing fruit each season. Their leaves never wither, and they prosper in all they do" (Psalm 1:1–3).

Here is your roadmap to happiness. What does God mention first in this Psalm? If we want to be happy, we must first understand that there are certain people we must avoid. We need to avoid the influence of "wicked" people. People who enjoy living a sinful life and hang around in groups of like-minded individuals. Those who take pleasure in making fun of others and demeaning the people around them then attempt to persuade you to do the same. It is true that the company you keep can and will often determine your joy or lack thereof in life. The best Biblical example of this can be seen in the parable of the prodigal son.

In this parable after the young man leaves home with his inheritance, he finds himself falling into a circle of "friends" whose example could have been pulled directly from Psalm 1. They reveled in their sin, they used people and discarded them when they no longer held any value for them, including the prodigal son. Did those friends bring joy to the life of the prodigal son? No, when the money ran out, they were gone. The son found himself alone, starving, and willing to do anything, even become a servant, to be surrounded once again by his loving family (Luke 15:11–31).

Step two in the roadmap towards joy and happiness focuses not on who you spend your time with, but where you spend your time. Those that spend their time in the Word of God, meditating on it and studying it day and night, find not just joy but prosperity for themselves, and the impact of that is felt not just by them, but by those around them as well. God inspired the writing down of His Word. It is His direction for life, for you! We just need to learn what He wants for our life, then learn more about our Father to find a life of joy and success.

How simple yet profound is this roadmap for happiness and success. Surround yourself with the right people and spend your time in the Bible. So, when you find yourself in those moments when you cannot find joy, life seems overwhelming, and happiness seems unattainable, then examine your life against Psalm 1. Are you with the right people? How much time do you spend on your relationship with God? God wants you to have joy; all you need to do is follow the roadmap He has given you.

Christmas

PRAYER

Dear God, we lift up to you our prayer on this Christmas Day. We offer you our praise and worship for your redeeming grace and the hope that was born on this day for all people. We pray that you would   fill our hearts with joy, hope in the one true God, love, forgiveness, and peace. We ask for the salvation of all our friends and family that do not know you Lord, and we pray for your blessings to flow to all people. Holy Spirit, fill us with your love and power so that we can shine the true light of Christmas, Jesus Christ, on all we see. In the powerful name of Jesus. Amen.

SONG

"Behold the Lamb of God"
by Andrew Peterson

Jehovah Jireh:
The Lord Provides

....

Matthew 2:1-18, Genesis 22:13

Jehovah Jireh is one of the names of God and it means "The Lord will provide." Have you ever had a moment where you needed something, and you prayed hard for it? Then, when it finally happened, it did so at just the right time? Or maybe you have been through a tough time, and it seemed like God was not there, or if He was, He was not helping. Then, after you made it through, you looked back and saw all the little things God did along the way. God provided for you, and you were not alone, he really is Jehovah Jireh, the Lord that provides. Maybe it was not how we expected, but when we look back over our lives, we will be able to see where Jehovah Jireh showed up and showed off.

One of my favorite stories in the Bible that demonstrates Jehovah Jireh is the story of the wise men after the birth of Jesus. Most of us know the story of the wise men, and most of us could probably name the gifts they brought of gold, frankincense, and myrrh. We may have even been told that the gift of gold is for kings, frankincense for priests, and myrrh for burials, intended to symbolize our Savior's death. Powerful symbols of priest, king, and Savior. However, these gifts were intended for so much more than a symbol; they had a purpose, and they were a provision!

The wise men arrived in Bethlehem roughly two years after the birth of Christ. Also, quick fun fact, nowhere in the Bible does it mention how many wise men there were, the number three came from a song written in the 1800s. Back to the story, once King Herod learned of Jesus's birth from the wise men, he ordered the killing of all boys under the age of two He did not want a new king to take his place. When the Magi (wise men) arrived to see Jesus, the gifts they brought were symbolic to the birth of Jesus as king, but they were so much more; they also were valuable. Without the value of those gifts Joseph and Mary would not have been able to afford to escape to Egypt, and Jesus would have been killed as an infant. But Jehovah Jireh showed up, and God provided. God put into the hearts of the Magi to bring specific gifts, not just to symbolize His son, but to save Him!

God's provision did not come on the day of birth, it came at the exact moment it was needed, nearly two years later. It came in a manner no one could have ever expected. A group of gentiles from thousands of miles away brought gifts that would provide the means to escape at the precise time needed. Truly an answer to prayer! So, when you celebrate Christmas think about the gifts of the wise men, not just for what they symbolized, but for what they provided. God gave provision at the precise moment it was needed most.

We all have trials and struggles in life, some of which seem insurmountable. In those moments remember you are a child of God, Jehovah Jireh! He provides hope, love, comfort, peace and so much more. At the time we need it the most, when everything seems impossible and we feel the most alone, take comfort in knowing God provides for all who love Him and are called according to His purpose. It may come in a way completely unexpected, but it will come in God's perfect timing. He provided for an ordinary couple two thousand years ago, and He will do the same for you. Have hope and share your love.

Peace on Earth, Good Will to Men

Luke 1:79, Luke 2:9-14, Isaiah 9:6, Isaiah 52:7, Micah 5:5

Suddenly, an angel of the Lord appeared among them, and the radiance of the Lord's glory surrounded them. They were terrified, but the angel reassured them. 'Don't be afraid!' he said. 'I bring you good news that will bring great joy to all people. The Savior—yes, the Messiah, the Lord—had been born today in Bethlehem, the city of David! And you will recognize him by this sign: You will find a baby wrapped snuggly in strips of cloth, lying in a manger.' Suddenly the angel was joined by a vast host of others—the armies of heaven—praising God and saying, 'Glory to God in highest heaven, and peace on earth to those with whom God is pleased.'" (Luke 2:9–14)

It must have been an overwhelming sight for the shepherds in the field that night of Jesus's birth. A host of angels appeared to a group of shepherds, who were considered unclean and often looked down upon by society, to announce the birth of the Messiah. From a life of despair to the promise of hope in an instant. From turmoil to a promise of peace on earth. Hope restored, prophecy fulfilled, and joy encountered in a chorus of angels praising God and announcing peace on earth.

One of the phrases that have long been sung in many Christmas songs is "peace on earth." It was sung that first night by a chorus of angels, and over two thousand years later we still sing it. Why? Because this is the promise of the Messiah, peace on earth. It is fitting to hear every year as a reminder of **what is to come**. No matter how desperate the situation, how bad the state of the world, or how deep the despair, there is always the promise of peace on earth with Jesus. There will be a day when he returns when the world will finally be at peace, and that is the reminder of Christmas. Peace on earth through Jesus.

It was mentioned seven hundred years before Jesus's birth when the prophet Isaiah prophesied about Jesus. "For unto us a child is born, . . . And he will be called Wonderful Counselor, Mighty God, Everlasting Father, Prince of Peace." (Isa 9:6, NIV). "How beautiful on the mountains are the feet of those who bring good news, who proclaim peace, who bring good tidings" (Isa. 52:7, NIV). The Israelites were in exile when they heard these words from Isaiah. Living in a time of despair, they were given hope for peace in the coming Messiah. From Isaiah to Micah (Mic. 5:5) to Zacharias (Luke 1:79), prophecy around Jesus often spoke the promise of peace to a world in chaos and despair.

That hope is still alive today, and around Christmas we find people's hearts more open to the hope found in Jesus, and we see the change in many. Consider the poet Henry Wadsworth Longfellow. In 1861, his wife was killed in a fire, and he was severely burned while trying to save her. In November 1863, his oldest son was badly wounded during a Civil War battle. His life had sunk into a pit of despair until

December 25, 1863. On that morning, he heard the church bells playing out a chorus of peace on earth, goodwill to men. What changed at that moment was not the circumstance. His wife was still gone, his son was still injured, and the nation was still at war. What changed was the remembrance of the hope and promise of peace on earth through Jesus Christ. And he authored a poem we still sing to this very day, "I Heard the Bells on Christmas Day."

So, we look to Jesus during this time of despair, conflict, and turmoil to be reminded of the promise of peace in Jesus. Longfellow said it well, "Then pealed the bells more loud and deep: 'God is not dead, nor doth He sleep; The Wrong shall fail, the Right prevail, With peace on earth, goodwill to men.'"

Yes, it Is Christmas, But What Is Advent?

Luke 1-2

When we think of the month of December, we think of the end of the year. It is the last month of the year and we may reflect on the year, but what if December was intended to be the month that reminds us of the hope we have **coming**? If we consider the season of Advent that takes place in December, that is exactly what it is intended to do. The Advent season starts four Sundays before Christmas, so it runs virtually all through the month of December.

If you have attended church services in December, there is a strong chance you have heard about Advent and seen the Advent wreath at a church with its four or, at times five candles. At the beginning of the service, someone will come up and light a candle and then read a passage of scripture. However, if you are like me, while the passages were excellent, I never understood why we celebrate Advent. And as a result, I never connected with the season. So, what is the purpose of Advent?

If you search the Bible for an understanding of the season of Advent, you will not find answers. Advent, as it is believed, started around the 3rd or 4th century. The word is derived from the Latin word "adventus," meaning "coming." We get a clue from this definition that it is about the future and what is to come. While it is not clearly known why Advent started, it was placed at the end of the church calendar to offer hope, excitement, and joy about what was coming, not about what had already come. For the early church, the season of advent focused on the second coming of Christ and the hope we have of Christ's return. It was not until the Middle Ages that the advent season also included reflection on Christ's first coming to earth at his birth. The Advent season symbolizes the present situation of the church in the last days as we wait for the return of Jesus Christ.

The scriptural readings will often focus on the birth of Jesus. However, the first two Sundays of Advent still look forward to the second coming of Christ, and the last two are intended to look back to the fulfilled promise in the birth of Christ. These four candles represent hope, faith, joy, and love; the verses read during these candle lightings will reflect those themes. At times there will be a fifth candle lit on Christmas day, which is to celebrate Jesus's birth.

The first candle remembers the promise of Christ coming in these last days. It is our hope in the promise of Christ returning. The second candle we light during the waiting. We are not unlike the Jewish people and the time between the Old and New Testaments when they were waiting for the Messiah, but all seemed quiet. We too are waiting with our faith to sustain us for Jesus to return. Then we shift to the lighting of the third candle. This candle is remembering the joy in the coming of Jesus as a baby and the verses of the announcement of his birth by the angels to the shepherds is shared. The fourth candle reminds us that God keeps his promises as he did with the first coming of Jesus, and he will do with the second.

The Christmas season has become so commercialized that the fight is often to remember the reason for the season, which is exactly what Advent is helping us to do. In the early church they would pray and fast during the Advent season to focus on the coming. Now with more insight into the meaning of Advent, we can focus our time each week on what God has done and that Jesus is coming, and never forget that this is a season of faith and hope about what is to come. Advent does not end our year, it starts our year off with hope, faith, joy, and love.

Devotionals

"All scripture is God-breathed and is useful for teaching, rebuking, correcting and training in righteousness, so that the servant of God may be thoroughly equipped for every good work."

2 Timothy 3:16–17 (NIV)

PRAYER

Lord, thank you for this time you have given me to study your Word and grow closer to you. Thank you for giving us your Word so that you are not unknown to us. You have revealed yourself to us through your Word, and in your Word, we can find your will and your will for our life. Please give me wisdom as I study, help me to discern your truth. Help me to lean not into my own understanding, but rely wholly upon you and the Holy Spirit. Amen.

SONG

"I'm Listening"
by Chris McClarney

A Man After God's Own Heart

One of the most talked about characters in the Bible is David. He was famous for defeating Goliath in battle as just a kid when the rest of the men of Israel were frightened. He was anointed as the future King of Israel despite being the youngest of all his brothers. He was hunted by King Saul who hoped to kill him and keep him from the throne. There are also many stories from his reign over Israel as well, but all these stories are tales we can understand. However, when the Bible tells us that David was a man after God's own heart (1 Sam. 13:14, Acts 13:22), what does that mean?

There are countless stories that demonstrate the faith of David, but David was not perfect; he failed as well. The most prominent of David's sins were adultery, deception, lying, murder, and pride. How could a "man after God's own heart" be involved in sins such as these? Surely, he would avoid sin and always live in a relationship with God. However, no man is perfect, so what can we learn from this sin? David's repentance, it is in his repentance that we see the heart of a man with a heart for God.

It was evening when David decided to walk around the palace, and as he was walking, he saw a beautiful woman bathing on the roof top of a nearby home. David immediately desired her, and once he determined who she was and where she was, he went to her and had sex with her. This woman turned out to be Bathsheba, the wife of one of David's close friends and military leaders, Uriah. After the adultery, she became pregnant, in an attempt to hide his sin, he tried to get Uriah to sleep with Bathsheba to suggest the child was not David's but Uriah's. When that failed, he had Uriah murdered in battle. Through all this sin, David struggled with the results of his sinfulness, but pride kept him from truly understanding how sinful it was until the prophet Nathan confronted him. History tells us that it was nearly a year later that David finally poured out his heart in repentance to God, and we can see all of this in Psalm 51.

Psalm 51 shows David's repentance and his desire to be washed clean from the guilt and purified by God. He acknowledges his sin against God and knows that only God can restore him. "Create in me a clean heart, O God (51:10)," he pleads to God. Remove the stain of sin, return joy to him, and do not take away God's spirit are all pleadings from David as the brokenness finally reached the point where he knew only God could restore him, and only God could bring their relationship back together. This broken spirit is what God was looking for, a letting go of the pride that led to David's sin and the pride that kept David from repenting. God wanted David's repentance and his reliance on only Him and not the world or himself.

What do we learn from this failed, flawed man after God's own heart? We learn that true repentance involves admitting your sins, revealing them to God, praising the greatness of God, asking God to purify you, clean your heart, forgive you and make your life a life of praise. We have all fallen short and sinned against God. Until we confess our sins to God, we will continue struggling like David. We will fall again and again to the same sin, and our guilt and sin will keep growing. It is not too late to ask for forgiveness. David's demonstration of a repentant heart is a powerful expression of love for God,   so powerful that David's repentance is still being discussed thousands of years later. He was a man after God's own heart because he recognized his flaws, and also identified the only One who could change that.

Remember the Source

Luke 17:11-19, Leviticus 14:12, Psalm 145:3

Often you will hear the word entitlement used to describe people, including whole generations. Entitlement means the belief that one is inherently deserving of privileges or special treatment. This is not a new problem, it has been occurring for millenniums, not just in millennials.

In Luke 17, we are given an example of entitlement versus praise. As Jesus was walking back to Jerusalem, he entered a village where he saw ten men. What was different about these men was that they all were suffering from leprosy. Because of their condition, they were required to maintain a distance between themselves and those without leprosy. So, they were at a distance from Jesus when they shouted, "Jesus, Master, have pity on us!" (Luke 17:13, NIV).

It was believed during this time that leprosy was a result of sin in the life of the leper. This is important to remember because they were now reaching out to Jesus as the Messiah to heal them from this disease. They believed God could heal them from leprosy, so when they saw Him, they cried out. Could you imagine all the pain in that sentence? Potentially decades of isolation of not being touched, not being loved, being an outcast, all because everyone believed you lived a sinful life and God was punishing you with leprosy as a result! "When Jesus saw them, he told them, 'Go, show yourselves to the priest.' And as they went, they were cleansed" (17:14, NIV). Two points to understand here. Jesus healed them without the need to even touch them. His power to heal has no limitations. Secondly, he had them report to the priests, this was an important Jewish law when it came to verifying that someone had been cleansed from leprosy (Lev. 14:12).

What is even more incredible is that no Jewish person had ever been healed from leprosy from the time this law was established until the time of Jesus. In fact, the only person recorded to have been healed of leprosy during that 1000 plus year span was Naaman, a non-Jew (2 Kings 5). The presentation of themselves to the priest would not only have established their healing but would have sent shockwaves through the Jewish community! Not just one person was healed, but ten were! But here is where the entitlement comes in.

Only one person of the ten came back to thank Jesus. "One of them when he saw he was healed, came back, praising God in a loud voice. He threw himself at Jesus' feet and thanked him—and he was a Samaritan" (Luke 17:15–16, NIV). The Samaritans were the despised enemies of the Jews, yet this is the man returned to praise and thank Jesus. Where did the rest go? Even Jesus asked, "Has no one returned to give praise to God except this foreigner?" (17:18, NIV).

They had all been healed, something that had never happened under the law, yet those that lived under that Jewish law did not offer praise or even thank Jesus. Apparently, they felt entitled to that healing. It took the Samaritan, the unlikeliest of the ten to praise the source of his healing, to remember from where his healing came. When we pray, we often ask God for specific answers in our prayer, but when he answers how often do we remember to praise Him and offer thanks? We are not entitled to or deserve His grace and mercy. He is our source for everything and deserves our praise. "Great is the LORD and most worthy of praise; his greatness no one can fathom" (Psalm 145:3, NIV).

Angels, What's Their Story?

16 Scriptural References in Body of Devotional

So, what is the story with angels? Are they real? What do they do? How often have you thought these very questions or had someone ask you something similar? There are many instances in the Bible where angels appear to deliver messages, but what else do we know? In this devotional, we will jump around the Bible and explore more about angels and their role.

What does the Bible tell us about the background of angels? We know that they were created before God created the earth. In Job 38:4–7, God is speaking to Job, asking how he can question God when he was not there when God laid the foundations of the earth, "as the morning stars sang together and all the angels shouted for joy" (Job 38:7). So, the angels were at the formation of the earth. They are responsible for carrying out God's plans, listening to each of his commands to do His will (Psalm 103:20–21).

They were among God's first creations, and when they were created, they were all good. "Then God looked over all he had made, and he saw that It was very good" (Gen. 1:31).

God created so many angels that they are beyond our ability to count. "Then I looked and heard the voice of many angels around the throne, and also of the living creatures and of the elders. Their number was countless thousands, plus thousands of thousands" (Rev. 5:11, CSB). Angels are eternal, the Bible tells us they never die in the Gospel of Luke. "And they will never die again. In this respect they will be like angels" (Luke 20:36). We also know that one-third of all angels chose to follow Lucifer and fell from heaven, these fallen angels are the demons of the Bible (Eze. 28:11–19, 2 Peter 2:4). They are not angels, they are fallen.

As a believer did you know that you have a guardian angel? When Jesus is speaking to the disciples about children he says, "Beware that you don't look down on any of these little ones. For I tell you that in heaven their angels are always in the presence of my heavenly father" (Matt 18:10). From this we learn two things: we have specific angels watching over us, and because God is omnipresent, those angels are always in His presence too. Maybe now you are wondering what the name of your angel is? Ask God to reveal it to you. I have known many people that have said God revealed the name of their angel to them.

Angels are our guardians sent to earth to aid believers as we follow God's purpose for our life. "Therefore, angels are only servants—spirits sent to care for people who will inherit salvation" (Heb. 1:14). They help in many ways: by answering prayer (Acts 12:5–7), by bringing announcements (Luke 1:13), by giving encouragement (Acts 27:23–24), providing protection (Psalm 91:11), giving guidance (Gen. 19:17), providing deliverance (Acts 12:7), and caring for believers as the pass away (Luke 16:22).

One of the best things we learn from the Bible about

angels is that sometimes they are with us, and can take on human form. "Don't forget to show hospitality to strangers, for some who have done this have entertained angels without realizing it" (Heb. 13:2). So, angels are real, and God has created them to watch over us and so much more. How much does our God love us that He uses His creation, His angels, to help us to achieve His will on earth? Think back now; have you ever entertained an angel?

What Is in a Name?

Matthew 1

If you have ever spent time reading the Bible, you've probably come across a long list of names, a genealogy. In the Old Testament it seems like just when the story is really flowing, along comes a genealogy. The names are difficult to pronounce, it is boring to read, the names often seem the same, and it is hard to understand the importance of this list, especially when for many in the list this is their only appearance in the Bible. There are long lists in Genesis, Exodus, 1 Chronicles, and Ezra, and then when we finish the Old Testament and turn to the New Testament and in the very first verse, we are thrust into another genealogy in Matthew chapter 1.

So, what's with all the names? First, it is important to know that the Israelites were very meticulous at keeping records. Look no further than the books of Leviticus for large sections of laws or the book of Numbers for constant counting of the different tribes, but not every genealogy from the nation of Israel is included in the Bible, so the ones that are included have purpose.

Genealogies were made to show the family lines through

the different tribes of Israel. This could allow a Jewish person to track their ancestry back to see if they were in the line of priests, or just as we do today, to see if they were related to biblical heroes such as Abraham and David. For a Jew, tracing your lineage to David or Abraham meant you were specially blessed because you are connected to the covenant between Abraham and God or to the line from which the Messiah would come in David. So, they were important, and they say so much more than just who begat who or who was someone's great grandfather. In Matthew 1, all of the purposes and meaningful importance in genealogy come together to set the framework for Jesus's ministry and explain how he fulfills prophecy as the Messiah through his ancestral line.

"This is the genealogy of Jesus the Messiah the son of David, the son of Abraham" (Matt 1:1, NIV). Right from the beginning the reader of this verse sees that Jesus is connected to Israel through Abraham, the one through whom God promised to bring blessing to all humanity. In Abraham's name we are immediately reminded of God's promise to rescue humanity, which is fulfilled when God sends the Messiah, who will be born through the line of David. Jesus is attached to the promise through Abraham and fulfills that promise in the line of David.

There are so many lessons that can be learned from the names of the genealogy of Jesus, but I want you to pay attention to four names that were not usually found in genealogy, and those four names were all women. It was uncommon to include women's names, and here we see the names of Tamar, Rahab, Ruth and Bathsheba. These names also were associated with scandals of adultery and prostitution and not all were even Jewish.

So, why include these names and not some of the beloved names of women in Jesus's line, like Sarah, Rebecca, or

Rachel? Because God wants us to see that He has used Jews, Gentiles, sinners, and outcasts to move His plan forward and that the Kingdom of God is for everyone. The preaching and teaching of Jesus and the message of the gospel in the New Testament is that God's grace and Jesus's sacrifice are for all, not just one group of people. Each name had significance, and for you and me, we are also included in the promise of God and the saving grace of Jesus Christ! And, we know that God will use all who are willing in His plan, Jew or Gentile, broken and unworthy, to bring every name back to Him.

Spiritual not Religious

Ever heard the statement, "That's not very Christian?" Sadly, it has been thrown around very loosely for many years. Whether you are being spoken to, or about, then doubt sets in. The question is a terrible judgmental statement. If you feel it's warranted to say, then you believe the lie of legalism, not religion. There are NOT specific steps to climb or fall as a Christian. There is sin, but ALL SIN is equal, and not one human is sinless!

Being a Christian is not about attending a certain church or claiming affiliation to one denomination. Being a Christian is believing in Jesus Christ, asking Jesus to come into your life, and believing that Heaven and Hell are real and that the only way to Heaven is through Jesus. He is the Way, the Truth, and the Life. John 14:6–7.

At times, the tasks required of you to participate in one church or another are simply modern legalism designed to "fit into" that building or group of people. If that is "your group," great! If it is not, then partnering with another group/ church can be just as beneficial. The church is intended to be a gathering of believers and non-believers coming together to worship God. The first century Christians were called this *ekklisía* and their intent was to worship, learn, live life together, and support each other through life's ups/downs. We need relationships that lift us up and help us through this thing called life! Galatians 6:1–3.

God's church does not have a list of requirements before it can be attended. It is open to everyone, no matter your circumstance or past. God desires to know you and to have a relationship with you, which happens through Jesus Christ. John 14:6.

People today want to be "spiritual" but not "religious." Absolutely, Be spiritual!

But first ask yourself the following question.

Who do I connect with to be "spiritual?" That search is open to all. One day, if you decide you want life in Heaven, then there is only one connection, and it is not labeled spiritual or religious. It is simply Jesus Christ.

Everyone that believes in Him will have eternal life, John 3:15. There will come a day when you will need to make a choice.

Seek to understand your "spiritual." Challenge legalism. Jesus came to seek and save the lost. He ate with the sinners. He ran to the sick and broken. He came to make a way for all people to have a relationship with Him.

As Christians, we have two steps for our spiritual walk:

First, believe in Jesus as your Savior, the connection by which you are spiritual, and surrender your life to Him. He is the ONLY Way to eternal life in Heaven.

Now, as a believer, go and make disciples. Loosely that means we have connected with our spiritual source Jesus, and now share how Jesus has changed you with others. Use your God-given gifts and help the less fortunate along the way. Simply put, we love God, love people, and use the passion inside us with purpose. Want to know more about that? Read more of our devotionals or watch our videos.

If you want that relationship with Jesus, you can do it now! Right now. Even if you have never talked to Jesus before, or it has been a long time, He is still there, waiting for you.

From your heart, simply say with honest intent these words. Jesus, come into my life. Make me brand new. Forgive me of my sins. Come walk with me Jesus, and show me how I can live and serve for you. Amen.

Why Are We Here?

Proverbs 16:4

Why are we here? Solomon, the wisest man defined in the Bible, advises us, "The Lord has made everything for His own purpose" Proverbs 16:4. If, we are here just to breathe and die, then why do we even exist? Well, that is deeper than we can take on at this moment, but you are here, here reading this, so let me ask you, why do you exist?

Do you get up each day for your spouse, for your kids, because you love your job?

What if all those were to go away, what would you do?

Science tells us we exist to evolve, so are you evolving? Are you becoming better than you were yesterday?

If you aren't, why not!?

Why let the world define you by what you do?

Do you know where to begin? Well, when was the last time you learned how to do something? How did you do it? Some of you magically may have "figured it out," but most of you went through training to do it!

So, what are you training for? What will make each day worthwhile?

As a believer in Jesus Christ, we are called to accept Jesus. I am the way, the truth, and the life, John 14:6. Then, we are to share our gifts and spread the news of Jesus (Matthew 28:19–20). Did you know you can do that right where you are, as a spouse, parent, office worker, factory worker, doctor, or teacher? What if caring for someone today in your world IS your purpose? What if just being the best YOU today WAS your purpose!?

Look at your day today; how can you see your PURPOSE in today, as caring for the person next to you at home, work, in the store or on the sidewalk beside you?

You have a purpose! You must only take hold of it and share it.

If you want to learn more about how you are naturally gifted with purpose that can be used to serve others, you must first study about your spiritual gifts and how your personality gifts are wired.

You are uniquely and wonderfully made, Psalm 119: 13–18. Take the UNIQUE you and use it to share the good NEWS with all the Earth, even if that is baking cookies for a new neighbor, performing yard work for an elderly person, or even serving in your local church. Wherever you feel the passion for helping those less fortunate, the "nudge" is for you to step. Be the hands and feet of Jesus, and bring people to know and feel His presence.

Go EVERYWHERE and tell EVERYONE, Mark 16:15 is for us today. Share your gifts!

Goal Setting

Did you know Goal Setting is biblical?

All the way back to the Old Testament, God asked Habakkuk to, "write the vision and make it plain on tablets, that he may run who reads it" (Hab. 2:2, NKJV).

Goal setting is an intention toward progress. In Proverbs 29:18, the wisest man known, biblically, Solomon, has written, "those without vision, will perish."

Think about it, when you don't know what you want to eat you run to fast food, which often leaves you feeling worse both physically and financially. If you don't know what to do, you sit on the couch, eat junk food and binge the flashiest show.

If you don't know where you want to go to conduct an activity, you become bored or let others dictate your day. This may leave you feeling neglected, unfulfilled, or even resentful that you "wasted the day."

Have you ever thought about how you learned a new task? Take riding your bike, for example, you'll have a parent or family friend with you to walk alongside you. You see the goal, riding without support on two wheels, being able to ride down the street all by yourself.

See the goal in front of you? You may not have written down the steps to get there, but the person teaching you knew the steps. They laid out the vision with you.

So how do you get to where you want to go? Some simple steps:

1. Write it down/or share with a person (accountability partner), where you want to go.
2. Lay out the steps to get there.
3. Run toward the goal.

What if you put that vision on a board, refrigerator, or bathroom mirror? Look at it every day. God tells us in Matthew 7:7, keep on asking, and you will receive what you ask for. Keep on seeking, and you will find. Keep on knocking, and the door will be opened to you. And Paul reminds us in Ephesians 6:18 to pray without ceasing.

Imagine if you wrote down what you wanted to work toward and looked at it each day. Then you prayed over the wording and steps and appointed someone to keep you accountable. Imagine what you can move forward toward!

Now, I am not saying your goals will always be accomplished. However, when they fall short, we MUST remember, His ways are higher than our own, Isaiah 55.

But, if we work to give ourselves a goal, if we line up the steps in front of us, and if we seek and pray for wisdom of wise counsel (Prov. 19:20.), then we WILL move forward.

It takes 3 weeks to make a habit and three months to make it a lifestyle. What if you started now? Where do you want to move forward in the next three months?

Write it down! And begin to move toward the GOAL!

What is your WELLness?

1 Thessalonians 5:23, 1 Corinthians 6:9

So, I want to ask, what is your level of Wellness.

According to Webster's dictionary, wellness is the state of being in good health, especially actively pursuing a goal.

Have you ever looked at a vintage car/ truck?

Maybe you like a 50's Ford truck. Perhaps a 1930s Cadillac convertible. Possibly it is a 1978 Trans Am!!

Now stop and think, what is your age? What kind of car are you? How about one that is the same age as yourself?! When you think of that car now, compare it to yourself!? Have you cared for yourself in the same way as that car? What if it has not been taken care of or refurbished? Yep, you see it.

As God says in 1 Thessalonians 5:23, May your whole spirit, soul, and body be blameless at the coming of our Lord Jesus. But, why don't we think about ourselves in a way that prepares our mind, body, and soul for blamelessness in the eyes of our Lord?

Now, when was the last time you cared for your body that well!? Do you regularly fill up with water to keep your fluid levels right? Did you know your body is almost 70% water?

Our heart and brain alone use 73% of water in our system to function! If we start to run dry, why do we fill ourselves with Diet Coke? If your prize vehicle were running low on oil, would you fill it with Vaseline?

How about another, do you put the right food in your body to make it run at top performance!? Do you put unleaded gasoline in your car? Why do you choose to run on bread and sugar alone!? What if your car overheats . . . do you pull over to the side of the road to "rest and cool down"? Do you wait till you are overheating to rest and cool down?

For all good cars to run, we are conditioned to take them in, get them serviced and work to prevent major repairs. Where is your maintenance schedule for YOURSELF? You, a high-functioning adult who works 60 hrs./wk., chase kids and engage in social life. Where is the maintenance schedule in your life?

Why do we take care of our cars better than we do ourselves? Why are we aware of the squeaks and thunks of our car, and we service it right away, yet we wait for our bodies to completely break or shutdown before we stop and listen?

Why don't we honor the body God has blessed us with? Our body is a temple of the Holy Spirit, who is in you, whom you have received from God. 1 Corinthians 6:19.

Start today! Get the hydration to lubricate your system. Eat the proper food to run at top performance. Sleep and relax to cool your engines and provide the best environment to reach your best level of wellness.

What if the best form of wellness for your body is prevention?

Today I ask you, what is your Wellness?

The Romans Road

Romans 3:23, 5:8, 6:23, 10:9-10, 10:13

Therefore go and make disciples of all nations, baptizing them in the name of the Father and of the Son and of the Holy Spirit" (Matt 28:19, NIV). Jesus commissioned every believer into the service of the kingdom. While we have many parts to play in this service, one that Christ specifically mentioned was for us to share the gospel message with the world. When we do this, we offer the opportunity for others to know Christ and be saved! We should approach this command to go and make disciples with a sense of urgency. No one knows when Christ will return, but we know that it could happen at any moment and so we have no time to wait.

For many of us the mere thought of evangelizing to people we know or even do not know is overwhelming! We do not know what to say. We are not sure of where to point them to in the Bible, and we may be worried we will mess them up. In this devotional, we will discuss the simplicity of the message and will also arm you with the verses in the Bible that present the road to salvation. If you can memorize these verses that is great, but if you cannot that is fine. Just remember that our call is to share the gospel, Jesus is the way. We can do that without knowing a list of Scriptures that share the story. Your testimony, alone, can do that!

The Roman's Road is the title given to a selection of verses in the book of Romans that discuss the need for salvation as well as the pathway to that salvation. They have been shared for generations, so let us look at these verses. You will notice that they do not always go in order.

Because we have all sinned, we are all separated from God. **Rom. 3:23** (NIV), "for all have sinned and fall short of the glory of God." And the price of sin is death, but God offers the gift of eternal life through the sacrifice of Jesus Christ. "For the wages of sin is death, but the free gift of God is eternal life through Christ Jesus our Lord" (**Rom. 6:23**). This gift was made possible by Christ dying for us while we were still sinners, demonstrating God's love for us. "But God showed His great love for us by sending Christ to die for us while we were still sinners" (**Rom. 5:8**).

If we repent of our sins and surrender our lives to Jesus as our Lord and Savior, then we will be saved from our sins. "For everyone who calls on the name of the Lord will be saved" (**Rom. 10:13**). It is the belief in our hearts, our faith in Jesus as our Savior that allows us to be reconciled and made right with God. "If you openly declare that Jesus is Lord and believe in your heart that God raised him from the dead, you will be saved. For it is by believing in your heart that you are made right with God, and it is by openly declaring your faith that you are saved" (**Rom. 10:9–10**).

The Roman's Road offers Scripture to show that we need salvation, all of us, and that it is a gift from God that demonstrates His love that allows us to live eternally. Jesus died for you, and if you declare your faith in Him and mean it with your heart, you will be set free from sin and restored to right standing with God.

If you ever find yourself leading someone to Christ, these verses will help tell the story. However, if you cannot remember the verses, you just need to have them say a simple prayer. Ask them to pray and repent of their sins, ask for forgiveness, ask Jesus to come into their life, clean them and make them new, and help them live a life that brings God glory. The message is simple, but the result is eternal!

About the Authors

Michael and Rachel Ferguson are a blessed and blended family of 8 with a heart for people. They have worked in the corporate world, in service for their local churches, taught in colleges, started businesses, and passionately seek to share Jesus. Michael holds a Master's in Biblical Exposition with over 20 years of experience in the Pharmaceutical Industry. He has served as a worship Pastor, interim pastor, and director of men's ministry over the years; as well as, served on several teams within the church. Rachel holds a Master's of Physical Therapy, and has been practicing for 20 years, coaching people through physical ailments. She is also a certified nutrition coach, wellness and life coach, and financial coach for both home and business. She is the founder and owner of Wholistic Wellness Services and serves on many teams within the church. Michael and Rachel enjoy sharing Jesus during their walks through their small town, online through media messages and devotionals, or wherever travel takes them with work and family. They strive to live a life where Christ is the center and foundation of their marriage, their family discussions, and their work conversations. You can check out more about Michael and Rachel and their ministries by visiting their website. www.ruahministriesinc.com

www.ingramcontent.com/pod-product-compliance
Lightning Source LLC
Chambersburg PA
CBHW040138160726
48006CB00014B/1533